C000004628

How to get the house you want

CONSUMERS' INSTITUTE OF NEW ZEALAND INC

How to get the house you want is a publication of
Consumers' Institute of New Zealand Inc,
Private Bag 6996, Wellington 6035, 39 Webb Street, Wellington.
Tel: 04 384 7963.
Fax: 04 385 8752.

Editor: David Hindley. Writers: David Hindley, Grant Hannis.
Cover design: Mission Hall Design Group.
Internal design and setting: Afineline.
Illustrations: Nicola Belsham.
Printed by GP Print Ltd, Wellington

ISBN 090 865 8-35-4

CONTENTS

Foreword

Section A: **BUYING**

Section B: **SELLING**

Section C: **AFTER THE DEAL'S DONE**

FOREWORD

Buying and selling a house can be a complicated and stressful business. You are confronted with the puff of real estate agents, the obscurity of the land transfer system and the confusion and doubt of offers and counter offers. But take heart. On the positive side there's the pride of having your own place which you can alter and decorate as you please; a landlord can't turf you out and you will be building up an asset. This will happen on two fronts. First, through paying off your mortgage and second, by the increase in the value of your house – between June 1986 and June 1996, real house prices in New Zealand rose by 33 percent.

How to get the house you want is authoritative, independent and comprehensive. It has been researched and written by David Hindley and Grant Hannis, two experienced and knowledgable staff members of Consumers' Institute. It is free from the influence of any sponsorship and this is what sets it above most other books. The text takes you through, in a logical order, the steps in buying or selling a house. But it does more. It covers holiday homes, timeshares and has a special chapter on housing as an investment.

The Institute is proud to be the originator and publisher of this book and I'm sure it will be a valuable handbook for anyone thinking of buying or selling a house.

David Russell
Chief Executive
Consumers' Institute of New Zealand

SECTION A: *Buying*

THE SEARCH BEGINS

You're ready to go househunting!

It's tempting to launch straight into it. The first few houses you see can be exciting, but if you've gone through 20 and have the feeling you're getting nowhere, your enthusiasm can start to ebb.

What you need is a plan of attack.

If you already own a house, consider whether there are changes you could make to avoid the need to move. Shifting house, even within the same town or city, can easily cost $10,000.

If you just want an extra room, then perhaps add one to your existing house; skylights and decking are cheap ways of transforming gloomy and tight spaces. See our chapter on renovations for ideas.

If you've ruled out renovation, then you still need to get an idea of your present house's market value. Do this with help from a real estate agent or registered valuer. Knowing what you're likely to get for your house provides a guide to what you'll have to spend on your future dream.

LOCATION

Location is more than just enjoying the view – it has a major influence on your lifestyle and your finances. Living beside a beach or in the hills some distance from your work can be a weekend delight, but it also means getting up early Monday to Friday for the long haul into town.

Work out where you want to live in relation to your workplace, schools, shops, leisure facilities, your friends or other family.

Travel can quickly put kilometres on your car's speedo, and whittle away its value. Public transport may be limited, or not available on weekends. But the quiet and the large section may be ample compensation for living out of of town.

No matter what your preference, buy in the best location you can afford. You've heard the old phrase: the worst house in the best street is a better buy than the best house in the worst street – simply being part of a good neighbourhood rubs off on the value of your house. It also puts you in the best position for capital gain: by renovating and tidying up the property, you can lift the value closer to that of other houses nearby.

Think about likely future values. Which areas are likely to become popular, which are declining? Real estate agents and valuers may help you here.

Whether you want to buy a new or existing house has a major impact on location. New houses are usually in new subdivisions, unless you can find a subdivided section in an older part of town. Another option is to buy a run-down place on a good site, demolish it and build a new home.

Use our location checklist below to help you choose the best location for your needs.

THE HOUSE

When thinking about your type of house, consider your present and future needs, lifestyle, and how long you think you may stay in the house.

Will you have children, or might your mother or father live with you? How often will you have friends or family staying? What are your hobbies? Our checklist below will help.

A major decision will be whether you want a new or old house.

New houses are usually well insulated, require little initial maintenance and have up-to-date kitchens and bathrooms. But on the minus side, they may be in new subdivisions with a garden needing extensive work, and rooms are often small.

Older homes may have larger rooms, more decorative features, established gardens, and be close to town. But they may also need renovation, more heating, and expensive maintenance.

If you plan to stay in the house for a long time – perhaps even retire in it – think about your future needs. Look in particular at access: in your later years you'll want easy access, low maintenance, good insulation, and so on.

Our checklist will help. Mark the items essential to you, and those which are just preferences.

The checklists

1. Location

Do you want to be close to:

- ☐ A dairy/supermarket?
- ☐ A bus stop/ rail station?
- ☐ Your work?
- ☐ Schools?
- ☐ Recreation facilities?
- ☐ Do you want views?
- ☐ Is it important that the zoning allows small businesses to run from home?
- ☐ Do you want to live on the flat?
- ☐ Do you want to be in an up and coming area?
- ☐ Do you want a quiet street?

2. Type of house

Do you want:

- ☐ A drive on section?
- ☐ A garage or carport?
- ☐ Sun?
- ☐ Low maintenance garden?
- ☐ Space for children/dog to play?
- ☐ Large rooms?
- ☐ More than one toilet or bathroom?
- ☐ Separate shower in the bathroom?
- ☐ Separate dining room?
- ☐ A quiet room parents can escape from noisy children?
- ☐ Low maintenance materials?
- ☐ Character?

HOW TO LOOK

Once you've sorted out the location and features of your ideal house, how do you find it?

You can do a lot yourself. Scouring local newspapers and the Property Press is a starting point. If you have time you could drive around likely suburbs and just see how many houses are for sale. This way, you'll see signs on private sale properties which a real estate agent can't take you to.

Newspapers and street signs can tell you when open homes are coming up.

If you're keen on an area which seems perfect for you, you could put leaflets in the letterboxes of houses which take your fancy. Make the note short and polite. Explain that you like the neighbourhood, and if they would consider selling, you'd like to talk to them. Give your full name and contact telephone numbers.

Local real estate agents can help. They know what's inside and behind the houses they list. They can save you time if they know exactly what you're looking for. Above all, they have a strong financial incentive to match buyers to sellers, and it won't cost you a cent.

SELL BEFORE YOU BUY?

If you already own a house, should you buy before you sell or sell before you buy?

The pluses of buying first:
- You have somewhere to move to.
- You don't have the cost of a rented house.

The minuses of buying first:
- You'll probably be making an offer conditional on the sale of your own house selling. Some agents are happy with this if they think they can sell your house without too many problems, but a conditional offer of this sort is less attractive to sellers. You may have to pay more to get them to accept your offer.
- You don't know exactly how much you have to spend, since your own home hasn't sold yet. Your expectations of what you'll get for your existing home could be too high.
- If you buy without selling your existing home, you'll face added expenses of bridging finance to buy the new house, or perhaps you'll be forced to sell your old house for less than you might otherwise have got, just to secure the new one.

The pluses of selling first:

- You'll have the cash to make an offer on a new home with fewer conditions. This makes you more attractive to sellers, so you're in a stronger position to get the sort of house you really want. As a cash buyer, you may get the property for a lower price than someone whose offer has more conditions attached.
- You can wait to get the best price for your property.
- You know exactly how much you've got to spend on a new house.

The minuses of selling first:

- There's a chance you may not find your perfect house right away. You may need to rent for a while – although the income from the proceeds of the sale of your old house can help offset this cost.

We haven't found any widespread agreement about whether it's better to buy or sell first. On balance, though, we think selling first is a good option if you can accept the chance you may need to rent for a while until your ideal house comes along.

Now that you know where you want to live and what sort of house you're looking for, you can start to consider individual houses. That takes a different sort of checking, as our next chapter describes.

2

CHECKING OUT A HOUSE

Buying a house, whether it's new or second-hand, is a clear case of buyer beware.

This chapter begins by outlining your legal protection as a house buyer. But getting redress if things go wrong can be difficult, time-consuming and expensive. It's better to check out a place yourself beforehand and refrain from making an offer, rather than buying a house and trying to seek redress later.

So this chapter also looks at the checks you can make to ensure that the property you're considering is as good as it's claimed to be. Some of these checks, which we'll look at first, usually apply equally well to sections, new and second-hand houses. Then there's additional information you should seek for sections and new houses.

You should carry out all these checks before you make an offer on a property – and then only after speaking to your lawyer. If several people are interested in a house and you don't have time to check the place before making an offer, make your offer conditional on all necessary checks. At the end of this chapter is a checklist you can use to assess any new or second-hand house.

We'll also look at different types of house ownership.

LEGAL PROTECTION

Under the Building Act, new houses must be safe and sanitary. The Act also requires that building consents must have been obtained for work done to a house (other than for very minor work). Previously, owners had to obtain building permits. If consents or permits weren't issued, the council can order that the work is demolished or brought up to standard. You can claim against the previous owner for the cost of this.

Houses aren't covered by the Consumer Guarantees Act. However, as a house is built the materials used in the construction are covered by the act (assuming the buyer of the house is the one who contracted for the house to be built). The materials must, for example, be fit for their purpose and be of reasonable quality. If a builder turns up with chipped roofing tiles, for example, you can demand they be replaced.

The Consumer Guarantees Act applies only to suppliers "in trade", not private individuals. So unless the seller is in the business of selling houses, he/she isn't liable under the act. But all the businesspeople involved with the sale (such as property developers, engineers, lawyers, real estate agents, valuers and builders) are. These people must supply their services with reasonable care and skill.

If you feel that materials aren't up to scratch or that someone in trade hasn't fulfilled their legal obligations, you can insist that things be put right, seek compensation, or, if the failure is severe, cancel the whole deal.

The Fair Trading Act also applies only to those in trade. This legislation states that you can't be misled about the house. You needn't, however, be told everything about a house either. Say, for example, that a house has rot. If the real estate agent doesn't say anything about the rot and you don't ask, you may have no comeback under the act. But if you specifically ask whether the house has rot and the agent says it hasn't, you can claim against the agent for misrepresentation. Depending on the severity of the problem, the whole deal might be cancelled.

Although private sellers aren't covered by this legislation, you could still make a claim against a private seller under common law for misrepresentation and the like.

Under the standard Agreement for Sale and Purchase of Real Estate used by real estate agents, house sellers have certain obligations. For example, the seller must have complied with the Building Act and there must be no outstanding rates.

But getting redress after you've bought a dud house may be difficult and costly. You're better off checking a place out properly before making an offer.

GENERAL CHECKS WHEN BUYING PROPERTY

There are a number of basic sources of information you should check:

- For a few dollars, you can obtain a copy of the property's certificate of title from the Land Titles Office at Land Information New Zealand (LINZ, formerly the Department of Survey and Land Information or DOSLI). This gives the property's legal description and its ownership history.

The title will also detail any encumbrances that exist on the land. These include easements – where another party has the right to use all or part of your property. For example, the neighbouring property owner may be allowed to lay drains under your section or build a driveway on part of it.

The title will also detail any covenants. These are conditions to which you must agree if you buy the property. These can include council conditions applying to the construction of houses built on the land – for example, that the houses must have concrete floor foundations.

Although most properties have straightforward titles, some strange things can turn up. For example, a covenant on a Wellington property prevents the construction of a fossil fuel heater in the house. This is because the downwind neighbour is an asthmatic whose condition is made worse by smoke. The neighbour and one of the property's previous owners had agreed to the covenant in the interests of the neighbour's health.

- If you have a copy of the certificate of title, the local authority can sell you a full land information memorandum (LIM) for the property. This gives information on such things as consents issued, easements, drainage systems, any potential instability of the section, any rates owing, etc. Prices for these can vary dramatically around the country, so ask.

- Contact your local city/district council and regional council and ask whether major roadwork and the like is planned for the area. The district plan will tell you what your neighbours are allowed to do (for example, how high they can build extensions to their houses). Ask, too, what new amenities are planned for the area.

  Enquire about zoning restrictions. For example, if you're planning to run a small business from home, will the zoning prevent this? Ask about the rates.

- Ask the seller to show you all relevant council documentation, including building consents (formerly building permits) and code compliance certificates. For details, see our chapter on having a house built. Make sure that all work that has been done around the property which required a consent or a building permit received one.

- You can obtain expert advice from a building consultant, architect or engineer. Expert inspections usually cost several hundred dollars. Check the Yellow Pages. The Building Research Association of New Zealand (BRANZ) also provides an inspection service through BRANZ-accredited advisers, who are independent technical consultants (For details ring 0900 380 80. In September 1996 calls cost $1.11 a minute).

Before hiring a consultant, ask them what they'll be checking and get them to show you the checklist they intend using to assess the property. We're concerned that some consultants don't use such lists. Also ask whether they have professional negligence insurance. If you purchase a house which received a clean bill of health from a consultant and you subsequently discover serious building faults, you could sue the consultant for negligence. You'll have a better chance of getting paid if the consultant has insurance.

- You can check whether the asking price is fair by hiring a valuer to give you an independent valuation of the property, and/or getting Valuation New Zealand statistics on recent comparable sales. See our chapter on valuations for more details.

- If you have any doubts about an engineering aspect of the property (possible land instability, for example), get an engineer's report. Use either a registered engineer, or an engineer who belongs to the Institution of Professional Engineers New Zealand (IPENZ). Both must be professionally trained and IPENZ members must work to IPENZ's code of ethics.

The address of both the Engineers Registration Board and IPENZ is PO Box 12-241 Wellington.

Engineers' and valuers' reports will cost several hundred dollars. Always shop around and make sure that the expert you hire is knowledgeable about residential property.

Check a house out yourself. You can use the checklist at the end of this chapter. The checklist can be used irrespective of whether the house is already constructed or still just in plan form (possibly with a show home example).

You don't have to be an expert to check out a house. But to do the job properly, wear suitable clothes and take a ladder, torch and screwdriver. In one instance, a couple couldn't check under a house because they were wearing good clothes. They bought the house anyway, but soon found bad rot problems under it, which would have been obvious if they'd looked.

When you're looking at the property, check the survey pegs. If you can't find them, pace the boundaries and check the measurements against the measurements in the title. This way, you know what you're buying. We know of one case where the boundary turned out to be many metres in from the fenceline, which meant that part of the house was on the neighbour's land. If there are any doubts, consider getting a survey done.

Buying sections

Look the section over yourself. Some potential problems may be self-evident. For instance, poor drainage and serious erosion will often be obvious after bad weather. To be absolutely certain, you can get an engineer to inspect the land.

Check out the sun and the slope of the section. Will the house you're planning to build fit on the section? Check out the soil quality. Is there shared access with other sections? If so, who will pay for and administer this?

If you have a copy of the certificate of title and firm plans for your house, you can also obtain a project information memorandum (PIM) from the council. This will detail any special features of the land known to the council (such as erosion, subsidence or flooding), details of any stormwater and waste-water systems and any statutory authorisations that must be obtained before building work begins.

New houses

You may be planning to hire a builder to build the place for you, or you may be buying a house from a property developer, such as a house building company. The following advice applies in either case. For simplicity, we've used the term "developer" to refer to a builder, house building company, etc.

First, ask the developer if the house construction is guaranteed. For example, through its member builders, the New Zealand Master Builders' Federation offers free Master Build guarantees on new homes. The guarantee promises that the federation will ensure that the building job is completed. If the job ends up costing more than the original contract price, the federation will pay up to five percent of the original contract price towards this. Also, any materials and workmanship which fails within five years is repaired free of charge. The guarantee becomes effective once you're issued with a guarantee certificate.

When you're looking around a new house or a show home, be aware that developers may use a number of tricks to make the place look more appealing. For example, developers may use light colours and mirrors to make rooms appear larger and striped wallpaper to make ceilings look higher. To make a show home look more spacious, there's often little furniture in the rooms and interior doors are sometimes removed.

Once again to check whether the asking price is fair, you can get an independent valuation from a registered valuer, who should be able to give an accurate figure, even if they've only got plans and specifications to go on.

Don't rely on a valuation supplied by the developer. There have been cases where the developer has provided inflated valuations.

COMMON PROBLEMS WITH EXISTING HOUSES

In 1993 and 1994, BRANZ surveyed over 400 houses in Auckland, Wellington and Christchurch to assess housing standards. On average, the houses' condition was rated moderate to good.

The survey identified a number of common housing problems. Keep these in mind when checking houses:

- House exterior and roof space
  - inadequate or blocked under-house vents, which can cause rot under the house
  - venting from the bathroom and kitchen into the roof space rather than to the outside
  - roof and wall cladding deterioration
  - problems with the foundations, including missing piles and unsafe excavations
  - missing or leaking spouting.
- Interior
  - unrestrained header tanks for hot water cylinders. These could fall or rupture in an earthquake
  - worn wall surfaces and fittings in the bathroom
  - worn woodwork in the laundry
  - worn wall surfaces in the living areas.

BRANZ said that all these problems can be fixed using existing building and repair techniques. But the cost can soon add up.

FORMS OF OWNERSHIP

Whether a house is new or second-hand, its type of ownership can differ, and this can have a bearing on its value. Make sure you understand the ownership structure of any house you're thinking of buying. The main ones are:

- Freehold. This applies to most houses. It means that the owner of the house also owns the section.
- Leasehold. You lease the property from the owner and pay rent.
- Unit title. Flats or apartments are individually owned but common property (such as the stairs and driveways) is owned and administered by all the flat owners together. Make sure that the unit plan sets out clearly both

the common property and the shared maintenance costs.

- Cross-lease. You own a share of the land and lease the buildings. Town-houses are often owned this way.
- Licence to occupy. This form of ownership, often used by retirement villages, means that you have the right to live there, but no right of title. Check to see what you or your estate gets when you leave the unit.

When you own property with others, there are two main ways in which ownership can be structured:

- Joint tenancy. This is the usual way. Ownership is shared and, on the death of one owner, ownership of the property automatically passes to the other owner(s). Most married couples do this.
- Tenants in common. You own a stipulated share of the property with one or more others. If you die, your share goes to the beneficiary named in your will (which may/may not be the other owners).

House checklist

General

New and second-hand houses

☐ Ask the developer, seller, or agent:
  - whether there are any protection orders over trees or buildings on the property
  - for the government valuation (a new house may not have one)
  - whether they have obtained all required building consents and permits and had proper approval for all work done; ask to see the documents
  - whether the house has a sewer or a septic tank
  - what fittings and chattels (such as floor coverings and TV aerials) are included in the price
  - does the property have stormwater drains

☐ Maintenance. Will the condition of the house and its construction mean that it will need a lot of work?

☐ Could the house be renovated?

☐ Speak to the neighbours. Do they have any disputes regarding the property you intend buying, or major plans for their property which may affect you (such as extensions to their house which will obscure your view)?

☐ New house only: What landscaping work will be required? Who will pay for it?

In addition, for second-hand houses

☐ Ask the seller or agent:
   – why they are selling
   – how much the rates are
   – when the place was last rewired.

☐ What repairs and renovations are needed now?

Outside

New and second-hand houses

☐ Can you afford the immediate work?

☐ Location – how close is the school, bus stops, shops, work, neighbours, etc.?

☐ Adequate street lighting?

☐ Road noise?

☐ Is the section big enough to be subdivided if you wanted to do so?

☐ Check the survey pegs. If you can't find them, pace the boundaries and check the measurements against those given in the title.

☐ Sun.

☐ There should be no gaps in the weatherboards or cladding to let in rain.

☐ Surface drainage. Is the ground landscaped and/or are there proper drains?

☐ Is the property likely to flood in heavy rain? Is it near a river?

☐ Are retaining walls sound? Are there any bare banks that should have retaining walls?

☐ Reasonable soil for gardening?

☐ Is there a carport, garage, parking? What is the access to the house?

☐ Are there lots of steps to the house?

☐ Is the clothesline near the laundry?

☐ Are there enough vents? An average 130 square metre house with a concrete perimeter needs around 28 vents, evenly spaced.

☐ Is the entranceway protected from the weather by a porch or canopy?

In addition, for second-hand houses

- ☐ Signs of excessive borer?
- ☐ Signs of damp?
- ☐ Weatherboards and outside walls. Could any problems be hidden behind fresh cement, paint or cladding? Tap suspect wood. If it sounds spongy and dead, beware!
- ☐ Get on the roof. Any signs of rust (or new paint possibly hiding rust) or cracked tiles?
- ☐ Look at the gutters. Any signs of rust or cracking, or fresh paint hiding this?
- ☐ Are the fences in good condition?
- ☐ Are any big pot plants hiding something?
- ☐ Make sure none of the vents are blocked.
- ☐ Check that metal flashings over windows and doors are not rusted.

Inside the house

New and second-hand houses

- ☐ Does the front door open into the living room? If so, this can allow heat to escape.
- ☐ Is there sufficient natural light?
- ☐ Are there enough rooms of the right size?
- ☐ Room layout: sun, efficient use of space, privacy, noise?
- ☐ Is the kitchen suitable? Is there a pantry?
- ☐ Check the quality of the TV reception.
- ☐ Adequate storage?
- ☐ Is the house insulated?
- ☐ If there's a header tank, check that it's securely fastened.
- ☐ All fans, vents and rangehoods should vent to the outside.
- ☐ Check the water pressure and plumbing by turning on several taps at once.
- ☐ Check that window and door frames are in good condition.
- ☐ Make sure the windows don't stick.
- ☐ Do the doors close properly?
- ☐ Are there enough power outlets?

☐ Ensure that gas pipes are working properly by turning on several outlets at once and making sure that the flame is strong and high.

☐ Check that all the chattels included in the sale are in good condition.

In addition, for second-hand houses

☐ Go into the roof space:

- any sagging, missing or dislodged tiles?
- bird's nests?
- any insulation? If so, is it in good condition?
- any cracks in the chimney?

☐ Any leaks, water stains, or suspicious new paint on the ceilings?

☐ Any cracks or bulges on the walls? This could be due to subsidence, moisture or condensation.

☐ Check wardrobes and cupboards for mould.

☐ Are toilets and cisterns in good condition?

☐ Is the shower and/or bath in good condition?

☐ Go under the house:

- check the piles. Are any of them missing or no longer supporting the house? Are they wooden or concrete? Wooden ones could be rotten under the soil line. Push a screwdriver into a few piles below ground level. Are they solid, or does the screwdriver penetrate the pile? If it does, the pile is rotten.

- look around: any floor problems hidden from above should be evident.

- signs of excessive borer

- signs of dampness, gaps in flooring, other problems.

3

THE BUYING BUSINESS

You've now decided that you definitely want to buy a place, and you've worked out exactly what sort of house and location will suit your needs. You also know the checking you'll have to do to uncover any hidden horrors in a property. This chapter takes you through the different stages of buying.

In brief, there are six stages:

1.   You look through a particular property and decide it's what you want, so you decide to buy.

2.   If it's being auctioned, you'll generally need to have finance arranged in advance. You'll also need to check the property thoroughly and arrange a valuation, since auction sales are unconditional (see below).

If the property is being tendered, you'll receive a copy of the tender documents, discuss them with your lawyer and get him or her to forward a written offer (see below for more details on tenders).

If it's a negotiated sale, you can make an offer to the seller. This is most usually done on the Agreement for Sale and Purchase of Real Estate form, a standard form prepared by the Real Estate Institute and the New Zealand Law Society. The seller or seller's agent will have copies. Get it checked out by your lawyer before you make a signed offer. If time is short, fax it to your lawyer and ask his or her opinion over the phone before signing.

You normally make an offer below the asking price, and perhaps with conditions attached. The seller may simply reject this offer if it's not enough, or the conditions are too restrictive. But if the seller thinks this could be a basis for negotiation, then he or she may make a counter offer. Usually, the seller puts a line through the price offered, writes in a higher price and initials this, then signs the document. The form goes between you and seller until a price is agreed on.

3.   Once an offer has been accepted and the price agreed, you pay a deposit (usually five or 10 percent of the purchase price). If the seller has used an agent, this money goes into the agent's trust account for a minimum of 10 working days. The agent takes his or her commission out of this money.

4.   If there is a long delay before settlement day, you could arrange a pre-settlement inspection to ensure all is as it should be, that chattels included in the sale have not been removed, the property remains in good repair, and any work promised by the seller has been completed in an acceptable manner. If there's a problem, consult your lawyer.

5.   At settlement date, you pay the amount to complete the purchase to the seller, usually through respective lawyers. Keys to the property are provided and you're free to move in. But talk to the agent or seller in advance about the time when the keys will be available. You won't necessarily get access to your new home the minute the money is handed over. Cheques take time to pass between lawyers. If settlement on more than one property is involved, that will also add to the time required for all the administration.

Settlement day is also the point at which the seller's insurance cover ceases and your insurance cover should begin. Arrange this before settlement day – probably at the stage the contract has gone unconditional.

6.   The formal paperwork for the transfer of title is carried out. In due course, your lawyer will send you a copy of the title document with the change of ownership noted.

It's not a difficult process, and having a good lawyer can make it even easier. But there are some aspects that you should understand clearly, particularly:
• What tender and auction sales mean
• What conditions you may wish to put in an offer
• What makes you a strong buyer.

TENDERS

Tenders combine elements of the ordinary negotiated sale, and auctions. Tenders may be open, or there may be a deadline date by which tenders should be received (a "closed" tender). A tender document is drawn up by the seller's lawyer, and this is given to you, the intending buyer.

You should then discuss an offer with your lawyer and make a sealed written bid to the seller's lawyer. This bid is effectively your top price, not a starting point for negotiations, so there are no second chances. It can, however, contain conditions. The seller considers the bids and either rejects or accepts them.

Advertisements for property tenders often set a price in such terms as "Offers over $200,000 are invited . . ." The process beyond this is private: unlike an auction, buyers keen on the property don't know what each other is bidding. If all tenders are rejected, nobody but the seller knows the prices offered. This means that, as a buyer, you need to think much more carefully about price.

You don't have to just pip the other buyers at an auction to secure the place, or negotiate hard with the seller. You must come up with a figure you're prepared to pay, trying to find a level that will secure the property without overburdening you financially. This is where valuations can be helpful.

AUCTIONS

Auction sales are unconditional. You must have your finance worked out in advance, and be convinced that the property you're bidding for is the one you want. You should have completed all the necessary property checks before auction day. A deposit, usually of 10 percent, is made at the time your offer is accepted. Most auction contracts allow attempts to sell the property before or after the auction date if it doesn't sell at the auction itself.

Most properties up for auction will have a reserve: the minimum amount a seller wants to receive. This isn't normally disclosed at the auction, though you'll often be able to work out the reserve during the bidding. An auctioneer may say "we're now on the market", or make some other sign that the reserve price has been passed. If the reserve hasn't quite been reached and bidding is slowing, this may also be obvious. An auctioneer may push buyers to go a little further.

If the reserve isn't reached but a bidder is close, the auctioneer may try to bridge the gap by negotiating with the seller to lower the reserve to meet the bid. There may even be a pause of a few minutes during the auction itself for this, if there's a likelihood of getting an auction sale.

It's not uncommon for properties which are "passed in" – that is, not sold during the auction itself – to be sold shortly afterwards. Offers may be conditional at this stage. The highest bidder gets the first chance to negotiate a purchase.

The idea of an auction is to build some excitement, to get bidders competing against each other and to secure the top price a buyer is willing to pay. You should also be aware, however, that to build this atmosphere a number of people who aren't serious bidders may attend the auction. The auctioneer may also have the right to accept bids on behalf of the vendors. These "phantom" bids aren't real attempts to purchase, but a technique to generate excitement and to get the bidding going.

If you're thinking of buying at auction, it's a good idea to attend a few house auctions in the early stages of househunting just to get the feel of how auctions work, to watch the different techniques employed to lift the price and to see how bidders operate. This way, if you see a property you really like, you'll be familiar with the auction process.

CONTRACT CONDITIONS

For negotiated sales and tenders, both buyer and seller can make the contract conditional. This isn't like an option: if the conditions are met, then you must go ahead with the purchase. Having a period when the agreement is conditional can, however, be very useful for buyers. It gives you a very good chance to look over the property thoroughly.

Among the most common buyer's conditions:

- Finance
  This allows the buyer time to arrange a loan to buy the property. To protect yourself, make sure that the condition has wide scope. The main way of doing this is to stipulate that the finance will be completely satisfactory to you. If the only finance you can find comes with an above-market interest rate and very high fees, then you aren't committed to the purchase if you have this type of wording. Your lawyer will know exactly what wording meets your specific needs.

  Contrary to popular belief, this clause is not inserted for you to be able to get out of a contract if you change your mind or see a better house elsewhere.
- Title search
  This means that your lawyer will obtain a copy of the title to the property and examine it closely. In most cases, the title is fine and this clause is just a formality. But it's a useful protection. The title may have some easements or restrictions on it which you're not happy about. With this clause, you're not committed to the purchase in such cases. Again, your lawyer will work out

the appropriate wording for this condition.

If you are buying a property on cross lease title, your lawyer should also look over the flats plans (see the chapter "What your lawyer does".)

- Land information memorandum (LIM)
  The LIM, which contains a wide range of information about the property, comes from your local authority. The LIM could show that part of the section was once an old refuse site, or that flooding can be a problem. Once again, this condition allows you to check out such things before the sale goes through. Allow at least 10 days for this.

- A builder or engineer's inspection
  This is most likely to be of use if you have some doubts about a construction. For example, the house may be built below a large retaining wall. You'd want an engineer to assess the wall and its stability before your contract to buy went unconditional.

  But since most properties contain some deferred maintenance, you shouldn't overreact when more minor flaws are pointed out. Often, the need for things like repainting or reroofing is reflected in the price of the property.

- Sale of the buyer's own property
  This isn't an attractive condition for sellers, but it's quite common. It means the sale goes through only when and if the buyers sell their own property. But if you're selling through an agent, the agent may be able to help here, by providing advice about how easy or difficult such a sale is likely to be.

There are also conditions which a seller might want to put in the contract. Two examples:

- Cash roll over, escape clause for cash or better offer clause
  Let's say you've made a conditional offer to buy a property, at a price the seller is happy with. Then, another buyer comes along who's prepared to pay the same price, but can make his or her offer unconditional. With this clause, the seller can give you a deadline (often three days) to make your offer unconditional. If that doesn't happen, the cash offer from the other buyer can be accepted. You miss out on the property.

- A particular settlement arrangement
  The seller might need longer than the average amount of time for settlement. For example, they may be building a house which won't be ready for two or three months. They can specify this as a condition in the agreement, allowing them to remain in the house for longer.

BECOMING A STRONG BUYER

To get the best chance of securing your perfect home, make yourself a strong buyer. There's nothing mysterious about this. You can do it by going through these steps before making any offers.

- Work out what you can afford. Take your calculations to a lender such as a bank, and get a home loan pre-approved to a certain level. If you already have a house, you could sell it first. This means that your offers don't have to be conditional on finance, and you can make auction bids.

- Find a good lawyer and discuss with him or her the fact that you're actively househunting. Ask that they give prompt attention to documents when you find a house you like. For example, if you want to make an offer on a property through an agent, deliver or fax the agreement to your lawyer before you sign, and ask for a quick response. This will mean fewer missed opportunities.

- Even if you don't want to sell your existing home first, at least get your property ready for sale. Keep it clean and tidy, and make any minor repairs or renovations which will improve its value. That way, if you want to make an offer for a property conditional on selling yours, the agent for the seller may be keen for the seller to accept your offer because your own place won't be too hard to sell.

- Know exactly what sort of property you want, and what your top price will be. Are you prepared to go up to your maximum price for immediate settlement, or if the seller is prepared to leave the plumbed-in whiteware in the house? Would you accept a delayed settlement if the seller were prepared to give a concession on the price? If you know your own mind, and you can convince the seller or the seller's agent that you're serious, they'll take you more seriously.

- Shop around and get to know the market. Read newspaper real estate supplements and attend open homes. Convince a buyer or an agent that you're a serious buyer, that you know what price the house you're looking for is likely to fetch on the market and that you're happy to pay that price.

4

WHAT YOUR LAWYER DOES

Whenever real estate is bought or sold, the ownership must be legally transferred. This is called "conveyancing" and is usually carried out by a lawyer. Both the seller and the buyer must have conveyancing work done.

This chapter explains how to choose a lawyer and what your lawyer will do for you.

CHOOSING A LAWYER

If you're thinking of buying property, contact a lawyer before making an offer. If you're selling property, your first step should be to contact a lawyer.

You don't have to use a lawyer organised by the real estate agent or your mortgage lender. Shop around. Ask friends for their recommendations.

Conveyancing is a very competitive field of legal work. We regularly survey conveyancing fees and we've found you can save hundreds by ringing around. Ask each lawyer if they're experienced in residential property conveyancing and for an estimate for your job, including GST and disbursements. Don't, of course, assume that the cheapest price is the best deal going.

Discuss your situation with each lawyer. Assess whether the lawyer seems knowledgeable and affable. Check whether the lawyer you're speaking to will be the one doing the work or whether a junior lawyer will be assigned the task.

To get an estimate, you'll need to tell the lawyers the price at which you expect to sell or buy the property and what type of ownership is involved.

Once you've selected a lawyer and the final deal has been struck, it should be pretty clear what legal work will be involved in the deal. You can therefore ask your lawyer for a quote. Usually you must pay your lawyer's fee before settlement goes through.

Part of the conveyancing work can include matters you're attending to yourself (such as obtaining a copy of the property's certificate of title, or organising the discharge of the mortgage). Tell the lawyer what work you've done or intend doing yourself. If the lawyer has less work to do, they should charge you lesser fee.

For a $100,000 house, you can expect to be quoted anything from $500 to $1,000 for a standard conveyancing job. There's usually more conveyancing work involved in buying a house, so buyers tend to pay more than sellers.

BUYING A HOUSE

Once you've selected a lawyer, ask to see the seller's proposed contract for sale. Sellers' real estate agents generally use a standard form for this. Insist on the most recent edition of the contract (when this book was written, that was the sixth edition, dated May 1995). Get your lawyer to check it out.

The lawyer will put into the contract any conditions that you want, such as making your offer conditional on all checks and finance. You can offer a lower price than the seller is asking and there may be a period of negotiation until a deal is struck.

Once a deal has been made, you usually must pay a deposit (often five to 10 percent of the purchase price) to the seller's agent. By law, real estate agents must put this money into a trust account.

Creditors can't claim money in trust accounts. This means that, if the real estate agent goes bust before your house purchase deal is completed, your deposit will be safe. The Real Estate Institute of New Zealand, to which all real estate agents must belong, also operates a fidelity fund. If the agent steals your deposit, you will be reimbursed from the fidelity fund.

To protect your claim on the property, your lawyer must obtain a guaranteed search document from the Land Titles Office. This means that for two weeks before and six weeks after the settlement date (the day the agreement of sale goes through), any claims on the property not noted on the title may be met by the government. Make sure your lawyer has the document. As a further protection, when the sale goes through, make sure that the title is registered straight away. Ask for a letter from your lawyer confirming that this has been done.

Your lawyer then sets about the conveyancing work. This includes:

- Obtaining a copy of the certificate of title. This ensures that the people claiming to own the land do in fact own it. It also picks up any encumbrances and covenants on the property. For more details, see our chapter on checking out a house.
- Obtaining a LIM and checking district plan requirements. Once again, for more information see our chapter on checking out a house.
- Preparation of a memorandum of transfer of ownership. This states that the property is to pass to you. The seller signs this and it goes to the Land Titles Office.
- Obtaining an assurance from the seller's lawyer that the property is free of other problems, such as outstanding rates.
- If need be, work with you to arrange mortgage finance and to ensure insurance is in place.
- If you are buying a property on a cross-lease title, your lawyer should check over the flats plans. This shows the position of buildings on the section, and details which areas are for the common use of all the owners and which are exclusively for one owner's use.

On the day of settlement, if everything is in order, the seller's lawyer gives your lawyer the keys and certificate of title, and your lawyer gives the seller's lawyer the balance of the purchase price.

SELLING A HOUSE

Discuss your sale with your lawyer, including any special conditions you want to add to the standard contract. If there's no standard contract, you and your lawyer can draw up a proposed contract from scratch, but this will be expensive.

Once the proposed contract has been drawn up, the buyers will consider it and come back with their offers. You may respond with counter-offers. This process can go on for some time. You'll probably discuss the counter-offers with your real estate agent, but you might want your lawyer's advice as well. You should seek legal advice before making a final commitment to any would-be purchaser's offer.

Once the deal has been struck, your agent will send a signed copy of the contract to your lawyer. The lawyer will obtain a copy of the certificate of title to check that everything is in order (for example, that there aren't any encumbrances on the property that will prevent the sale).

Your lawyer will deal with the buyer's lawyer to ensure that all the conditions of the deal have been fulfilled.

If you have a mortgage, your lawyer will organise for it to be discharged. The lawyer will also ascertain how much you must repay the lender. If this is more than the purchase price will cover, you must pay the balance.

The lawyer will prepare a settlement statement, which is sent to the buyer's lawyer, detailing which party must pay rates and any other costs (such as unit title levies).

On the day of settlement, if everything is in order, your lawyer will receive the balance of the purchase price and send your copy of the title and other appropriate documents to the buyer's lawyers. Your lawyer will then pay any mortgage owing, give you the balance and send a notice of change of ownership to Valuation New Zealand.

When you're selling your house, don't forget to arrange to have the gas, electricity and telephone cut off and have regular rates payments stopped. Unless your lawyer sees to it, you'll also have to cancel your house insurance and organise a final water meter reading. Send redirection notices to New Zealand Post and cancel the newspaper.

NON-LAWYER CONVEYANCING

You don't have to use a lawyer for the conveyancing work. To save money, some people do the work themselves. This means working through the various steps outlined above. Do this only if you feel confident that you can do the job properly. Getting it wrong can be expensive to fix.

There are also some non-lawyer conveyancers around. For more information on non-lawyer conveyancing, contact the New Zealand Institute of Conveyancers Inc. (PO Box 6800, Wellesley Street, Auckland 1). This organisation has developed from a similar one in Australia, where non-lawyer conveyancing is relatively common.

5

MORTGAGES

For most people, buying a house is the biggest purchase they ever make. It's no wonder they usually have to borrow money to manage it. This chapter explains how to find the best mortgage for you and how to pay it off as quickly as possible.

DEFINITIONS

Before we go any further, a few definitions.

When you want to borrow money to buy a house, the lender usually secures the loan over the property. The document that secures the property is called the "mortgage". The legal documentation will refer to the "mortgagor" (that's you, the borrower) and the "mortgagee" (the lender).

Most people also use the term "mortgage" to describe the loan itself. Given the widespread use of the term in this way, we'll do the same (although, strictly speaking, the loan is simply that – a loan).

Lenders typically lend only a certain percentage of a house's value (usually up to 75 to 80 percent, although some lend up to 95 percent). The amount you borrow is called the "principal".

You must front up with the rest of the money yourself. Most people refer to this as their "deposit", and we'll do likewise, although the money you put into the house is really your initial equity. The deposit is the money you give the real estate agent to confirm your offer to buy a house (usually five to 10 percent of the purchase price).

GETTING A LOAN

Mortgages are available from a wide variety of sources, including banks, building societies, insurance companies, even solicitors. Banks, though, are the main source.

Banks are very keen to provide mortgage finance. It's a low-risk, simple form of lending. The market is very competitive and banks offer a wide range of well-priced flexible products. Contacting the banks is easy; just pick up the phone. Many banks have toll-free telephone infolines, where you can learn about the types of mortgage the bank offers and its interest rates.

You shouldn't feel nervous or awkward about doing this. Banks are used to people ringing up asking about mortgage deals. The days are gone when you needed to have a long savings record with a bank to get a home loan. In fact, some banks even offer conditional loan approval over the phone.

Usually, though, you'll need to visit the bank to discuss the details of your loan application. Some banks, however, have mobile mortgage managers who will come to you.

When applying for a loan you'll need to provide at least the following information:

- The amount you have for your deposit.

  Usually you must contribute at least 25 percent of the house's price yourself, but a lender may lend you more than 75 percent of the house's price, albeit sometimes at a higher interest rate.

- How much you want to borrow.

  As well as the balance of the purchase price, this can include the costs associated with buying (the lawyer's and valuer's fees, the loan administration fee, moving costs, etc.). On a house requiring a $100,000 loan, these additional costs can easily run up to $3,000 or more.

- Your age, occupation and gross income.

  Bring along some bank statements or a letter from your employer to prove how much household income you earn. If you plan to have a house-mate whose rent will help to pay your mortgage, sound out potential house-mates on what rent you could charge.

- Your estimated household budget, including your living costs, insurance, debt repayments, car, etc.

  Usually the banks can tell you very quickly whether they will lend you money, how much and the loan term. This is often driven by your budget. Generally, your repayments can't exceed 25 to 30 percent of your gross household income.

To see the repayments you'd have to make on a mortgage, you'll find a guide at the end of this chapter, which explains how to do the calculations. Of course, you can also discuss the possibilities and different repayment requirements with the bank.

If one bank offers you a good deal, challenge other banks to better it. We know of cases where customers have been surprised by just how far banks are prepared to go to get their business.

Some banks will also provide a mortgage guarantee certificate – a document stating how much the bank has agreed to lend you. This can be a very useful bargaining tool when discussing prices with the seller of a house. Guaranteed finance is as good as a cash offer.

Mortgage brokers

As well as contacting banks directly, you can use mortgage brokers (sometimes real estate agents can recommend brokers, or you can consult the Yellow Pages). Some mortgage brokers are paid a commission by the lender for any mortgage they organise; other brokers charge you. Make sure you know exactly how a broker charges his or her fee and how much the fee is. Read the fine print!

The broker may arrange a variety of deals or specialise in a few areas such as short notice loans. As with a bank, you provide the broker with information on your financial situation. Providing you meet the criteria, the broker will come up with a lender or lenders that can supply you with finance.

If you've been to some lenders directly and they've turned you down, a broker may be able to organise finance for you. Make sure, though, that any such deal won't leave you financially overstretched.

Using a broker has its advantages. The broker does the phoning around to set up the mortgage, saving you time and hassle. And a broker may also organise valuations and provide you with legal and insurance advice.

But there can be disadvantages. The broker may represent only a few lenders, so you may not get the best deal available. Also, unless the broker is clearly an agent of a bank, a broker will not be covered by the Banking Ombudsman. If things go wrong, you may have to initiate costly court action.

We recommend that you use a broker simply as another possible source of finance. Contact some mortgage lenders directly and see what they offer. Then contact some brokers and see what deals they can put together. Compare the alternatives and make your choice.

If you're paying the broker, don't pay until the mortgage has been finalised and your lawyer has checked that everything is in order.

Insurance and defaulting

Mortgage lenders usually insist that you insure the house, but usually allow you to have either indemnity or replacement cover.

Lenders don't usually require you to have mortgage repayment insurance. This is because the loan is secured by the house. If you default, the lender can step in and sell the place to recoup the loan. This is known as a "mortgagee sale". But lenders normally do this only as a last resort. If you're having trouble repaying the mortgage, speak to the lender as soon as possible. It's likely the repayments can be restructured to meet your budget. For example, the term of the loan may be extended, which will reduce the regular repayments (but will mean that you pay more interest overall).

In some cases, a lender may require you to have mortgage repayment insurance, especially if you're borrowing a high proportion of the house's value. That's because, if you default, the mortgagee sale may not recoup all the money you owe the lender. In some cases, the insurance is in your name, in others the bank's.

Although lenders may not require it, we think you should have the mortgage repayments insured. This will avoid the family house being sold if the breadwinner can no longer pay the mortgage because of death, disability or loss of job. You don't have to use mortgage repayment insurance for this. Your life could be insured using term life insurance for example, and your income using income protection insurance.

Several banks offer mortgage repayment insurance, but they can't force you to take their insurance as part of the mortgage deal. Other banks and insurers also offer this insurance, so shop around and compare prices and cover. Some policies cover you only if you die or are disabled. Others also cover you if you're unemployed (but these, of course, are more expensive). Check the definition of disablement used in the policies too.

TYPES OF MORTGAGES

There are three types of mortgage:

- Table.

  These are the most common. Repayments don't alter over the life of the mortgage. At first, the repayments are nearly all interest with very little of the principal being repaid. Over time, however, principal is repaid, which means there's less interest to pay. Progressively, more of each repayment is made up of principal.

- Reducing.

  You pay back an equal amount of principal each time, with the balance of the repayment comprising interest. As the principal is reduced with each repayment, so the interest payable reduces. This means that each repayment is less than the previous one.

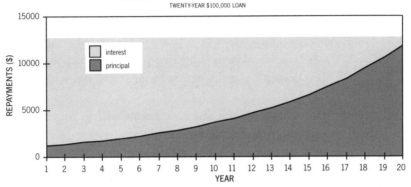

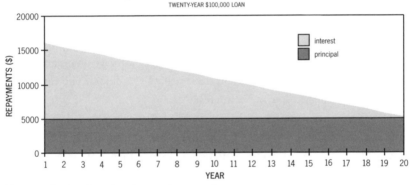

These graphs show how these two mortgages work

- Flat (or interest-only).

  You repay no principal during the term of the loan, only interest. The principal is repaid at the end of the term. These mortgages are usually provided only as bridging finance.

  Some time ago, several New Zealand lenders began offering endowment-linked mortgages, which link your mortgage to a life insurance investment product (which is used to pay off the principal at the end of the term). This is an expensive and risky way of borrowing money and we don't recommend it.

  On a mortgage, the standard lender's fee is one percent of the principal. Check whether there are other fees. The lender's fee can be built into the mortgage, but that means you'll pay interest on it. This fee is sometimes negotiable. For example, if you buy your house insurance from the bank at the same time, the fee may be reduced. Also, lenders run promotions from time to time waiving the fee altogether.

Which is cheapest?

Say you have a $100,000 mortgage, an interest rate of 11.5 percent, monthly repayments and a term of 20 years.

The most expensive option would be a flat mortgage. The total interest bill would be $230,000. Next would be the table mortgage, with a total interest bill of $155,943. The cheapest option is the reducing mortgage, with a total interest bill of $115,480.

But comparing mortgages in this way is rather misleading. For one thing, the differences in the total interest bills for the three mortgage types reflect the different repayment structures. A flat mortgage may mean the highest total interest bill, but it also means you get the use of all the principal for the entire 20 years. You must pay for that.

Also, if you can afford to maintain the high initial repayment of the reducing mortgage, $1,375, you would be better off taking out a table mortgage. In our example, this will reduce the term to 10.5 years and the total interest bill to $72,122. Compared to the reducing mortgage, that's a saving of $43,357 in interest. It's just common sense really – the quicker you can pay off the mortgage, the less you pay in interest.

(For simplicity, throughout this chapter we haven't included inflation in our calculations, but you should remember that, the further into the future you're making savings, the more inflation will erode their real value.)

Floating, capped and fixed rates

As well as different types of mortgages, lenders also offer different types of interest rates:

• Floating

Here the interest rate can be altered at any time. Because the funding of floating-rate mortgages often comes from the wholesale money market, changes in floating rates are driven largely by changes in wholesale money market rates. These, in turn, are driven by factors such as the Reserve Bank's monetary policy stance and international investment trends.

• Fixed

The interest rate is fixed for a period of time, usually one to three years.

Fixed rates are typically set below floating rates and involve a gamble between you and the bank. If during the period when your fixed rate is locked in floating rates stay the same or rise, you're laughing.

But if floating rates fall below your fixed rate, you're paying more than a floating-rate customer. Whether you end up worse off overall will depend on how long floating rates remain below fixed rates and how far they fall. For example, assume that eleven months into a one-year fixed term, floating rates drop marginally below the fixed rate. For the twelfth month, the fixed-rate borrower will be paying more than the floating-rate borrower. However, it's likely the savings the fixed-rate borrower enjoyed in the previous eleven months will more than compensate for this.

Fixed-rate mortgages are more inflexible than floating-rate mortgages. During the period the rate is fixed, you may be unable to make extra repayments or to repay the mortgage early, or you may only be able to do so by paying a fee.

When you're investigating mortgage deals, ask the banks what happens to the mortgage at the time the fixed-rate period ends. In some cases, fixed-rate mortgages automatically become floating ones. But, in other cases, you have the option of rolling your mortgage over to one of the fixed rates prevailing at the time. This option may be free or may incur a fee, so check it out.

Whereas all banks tend to charge the same floating rate, different banks often charge different fixed rates, so it's worthwhile shopping around. Looking at the three-year rates, for example, we found one bank offering a fixed rate over one percentage point less than another bank. Assume you want to borrow $100,000 on a table mortgage. At 11.5 percent per annum, you'll pay $3,778 more in interest during the three-year period the interest rate is fixed than if you'd borrowed at, say, 10.25 percent per annum.

Fixed-rate mortgages are popular. According to a 1996 Real Estate Institute survey, 70 percent of new home-loan lending was at a fixed rate.

- Capped

In a sense this rate offers the best of both worlds. The interest rate can drop if floating rates drop below the capped rate, but can't rise above the cap, even if floating rates do. The starting rate for a capped mortgage will be higher than for a fixed one, because you aren't taking the same gamble. Capped-rate mortgages can be more flexible than fixed-rate ones.

But few banks offer capped rates. In August 1996, we found only 3 banks that offering them. Another bank had recently stopped offering capped rates because, it told us, the product was no longer viable.

Once again, shop around. Let's assume the capped rate doesn't change for the year it's in force. If you borrow at 11.5 percent per annum, you'll pay $1,003 more in interest over that year than if you'd borrowed at 10.5 percent.

Fixed and capped mortgages offer certainty. You know how much of your household budget must be set aside for the mortgage. This certainty is particularly valuable for first-time home owners on tight budgets. With a floating-rate mortgage, you're constantly aware that interest rate rises could blow your budget.

Some commentators argue that banks treat fixed and capped-rate mortgages as potential loss leaders; in other words, they offer these mortgages to attract new customers, and are prepared to risk losing money on the deal. Whether this is true or not, we think that, when you're shopping around for a mortgage, you should seriously consider a fixed or capped mortgage.

Before we discuss that issue though, let's look at how you can re-structure a floating-rate mortgage, the most flexible mortgage option, to save money.

REDUCING THE COST OF A FLOATING-RATE MORTGAGE

Our examples use a table mortgage.

Changing repayments

Most mortgage lenders allow you to change your repayments without penalty. So, if you find you can no longer afford to maintain repayments at their current amount (for example, you become a single- rather than a double-income family), talk to your lender about reducing your repayments. If you do this, remember that the term of the loan will lengthen and this will increase the total interest bill. Lenders, too, have a maximum term (often 25 or 30 years).

If your financial situation takes a turn for the better – say, for example, you move to a higher paid job – you can make big savings on your mortgage by increasing the mortgage repayments. If you have a $100,000 table mortgage, at 11.5 percent interest per annum, over a term of 20 years, the monthly repayment is $1,066. The total interest bill is $155,943.

If, after five years, you increase your monthly repayment by $200, the term drops to 15.5 years and the total interest bill to $119,842.

Interest rate changes

When interest rates change, one of two things can happen:
• You can start paying a new repayment so that the mortgage is paid off at the same date it would have been paid off under the old interest rate, or

- You can continue to pay the same repayment, which will alter the term of the mortgage.

When the interest rate falls, you can save money by keeping the repayments at the same level they were previously.

Back to our $100,000 table mortgage over 20 years at 11.5 percent per annum. The repayment is $1,066. If, after five years, the interest rate fell to 10.5 percent, the monthly repayment required to pay off the mortgage in 15 years (that is, the balance of the 20-year term) would be $1,009 and the total interest bill across the 20 years would be $145,625. But if you kept the repayment at $1,066, the term drops to just over 18 years in total and the total interest bill is $133,205.

Repayment frequency

Many people repay a mortgage monthly. But you can make big savings by paying half your monthly repayment fortnightly. This is because there are 26 fortnights in a year but only 12 months. In effect, you're making an extra monthly repayment each year.

Let's look again at our 20-year table mortgage at 11.5 percent. By paying half the monthly repayments fortnightly, the term drops to 15.5 years and you save $42,203 in interest.

Pay off early

If you receive an inheritance or a rise in income, spend what you can on paying off the mortgage.

This is because paying off a debt is equivalent to making a relatively high return on a low-risk investment. If the mortgage interest rate is 11.5 percent per annum, paying off the mortgage is approximately the same as making an investment at 11.5 percent per annum after tax.

For example, assume you receive a $5,000 inheritance when you're five years into paying off a 20-year $100,000 table mortgage at 11.5 percent per annum. If you invested the $5,000 at 8 percent per annum paid monthly (before tax at 33 percent), in one year you would have earned $275 after tax in interest. But if you used the $5,000 as a lump sum repayment on the mortgage, you would have saved $606 in interest over that year. You're $331 better off.

Most lenders charge no fees for paying off early or for making lump-sum repayments on a floating-rate mortgage. Occasionally, though, there are special conditions, so it pays to check.

On fixed-rate mortgages, lenders may charge penalties for lump sum or early repayments during the period the rate is fixed.

Revolving credit

If you establish a revolving credit facility on your mortgage, you can borrow against your house's value at any time and repay when you like. You can reuse this facility as you please.

This is simpler and quicker than organising new loans from your lender. Also, the revolving credit interest rate is lower than interest rates on overdrafts and personal loans. There may be other fees on the revolving credit facility, such as an application fee and an annual maintenance fee. Make sure you understand all the fees.

So far, we've been looking at how to save money on a floating-rate mortgage. But a new borrower may be considering taking out a fixed- or capped-rate mortgage. Is this a better option? We think it may be.

TAKING THE GAMBLE

With a fixed-rate mortgage you're taking a punt that floating rates won't soon drop below the fixed rate and/or drop a long way below fixed rates. That's a gamble, but over the past few years those who've taken the risk have ended up saving money.

Let's say three customers each borrow $100,000 for 20 years at the average fixed rate in January – one in 1993, the next in 1994 and the last in 1995. Compared with what they'd have paid in interest on a floating mortgage that year, the 1993 customer would have saved $766 in interest. The 1994 customer would have saved $1,464. But the 1995 customer would have saved only $303.

This, despite the fact that for two short spells during this period floating rates fell below fixed rates.

We emphasise that these calculations are based on average interest rates, and are indicative only.

Will this trend continue? That's hard to say. Forecasting whether it's going to rain tomorrow is hard enough, let alone forecasting mortgage rates over the next 20 years! Although economists' predictions are scorned by some, they're the best information we can go on. The following calculations are based on the most recent figures available in August 1996.

The future

The NZ Institute of Economic Research (NZIER) has forecast that the average floating rate will gradually decline to 9.8 percent per annum by March 2000. The NZIER forecasts quarterly average mortgage rates, which don't pick up short-term interest rate volatility.

On a $100,000 loan, we calculated the total interest for a 20-year $100,000 mortgage at NZIER's predicted floating rates, and compared this with the interest on the current average fixed rates for one and three years, and the current average one-year capped rate. Once the fixed and capped rate period expires, the mortgages revert to the forecast floating rate. Interest rates were assumed not to change beyond the end of the forecast period, March 2000.

The one-year capped rate produced a total interest saving of $215. The one-year fixed rate would save $853. The three-year fixed rate saved $1,276.

Existing borrowers

If you're taking out a new mortgage, it's pretty clear that a fixed rate can be an attractive proposition. But if you already have a floating-rate mortgage, is a switch worthwhile?

We think it is, particularly if, when you make the switch from floating to fixed, you keep your repayments at the same level. This is because you'll repay principal earlier. The effect can be striking.

Take our $100,000 mortgage example using the NZIER's forecast rates. Assume a 20-year mortgage starting at an average floating-rate of 11.5 percent per annum. The monthly repayment would be $1,066. If you switched to a fixed rate of 10.6 percent for one year (which then returned to the floating rate), the repayment for that year would drop to $1,005. The saving in interest over the 20 years would be $215.

But if you kept the repayments on the fixed mortgage the same as the initial repayment of the floating mortgage for the first year, the term of the loan would drop slightly and the interest savings rise to $5,566. This greater saving is achieved simply because you're repaying more of the mortgage earlier.

Conclusion

The evidence suggests that you can take the best advantage of fixed-rate mortgages if you're a new mortgage borrower, or an existing mortgage holder prepared to stay with the same mortgage lender and keep your repayments at the same level.

We emphasise that fixed-rate mortgages do involve a risk: floating rates could fall below your fixed rate during the period it's fixed. Capped mortgages remove the risk, but they also offer smaller rewards. Don't forget that fixed-rate mortgages can be inflexible in other ways; for example, you often can't alter repayment amounts.

To calculate the interest savings you might make on your mortgage isn't a simple task. We suggest you discuss the options with your lender, who can tell you the likely costs and savings.

Calculating mortgage repayments

The general formulas are given below. The actual amount you will pay may vary owing to fees, mortgage repayment insurance and so on.

In all of our examples, we use a $100,000 mortgage, an interest rate of 11.5 percent per annum, monthly repayments and a term of 20 years. Before we look at the repayments for the different types of mortgages, we'll need to calculate two figures:

A. The periodic interest rate. To calculate this, we first divide the percentage interest rate per annum by 100. This expresses the percentage interest rate as a decimal. We then divide this by the number of repayments per year. Our interest rate per annum is 11.5 percent pa, and there are 12 repayments each year (ie, repayments are monthly). Expressed as a decimal, the interest rate is 11.5/100 = 0.115. The periodic interest rate is therefore 0.115/12 = 0.0095833. Jot this down on a piece of paper.

B. The total number of repayments across the term of the loan. This equals the number of repayments per year multiplied by the number of years. In our case, this is 12 repayments per year over 20 years, i.e. 12 x 20 = 240. Jot this on a piece of paper too.

Table mortgage

To work out table mortgage repayments you will need a calculator that has a +/- button and a y^x (or x^y) button. Most scientific calculators have these.

A. Take the periodic interest rate and add 1. In our case, this makes 1.0095833. Leave this number sitting on your calculator screen.

B. Now press the y^x button, enter the total number of repayments across the term, press the +/- button, and then press the = button. In our example, this raises 1.0095833 to the power of -240. The result is the number 0.1013636. Jot this down.

C. Now subtract from 1 the number arrived at in step B. In our example, this is 1 − 0.1013636 = 0.8986364. Jot this down.

D. Now divide the periodic interest by the number achieved in step C. In our example, 0.0095833/0.8986364 = 0.0106642. Leave this number sitting on your screen.

E. Finally, multiply the number achieved in step D by the principal. In our case, it is 0.0106642 x $100,000 = $1,066.43. This is the monthly repayment for a table mortgage.

Reducing mortgage

A. Divide the principal by the total number of repayments across the term of the loan. In our case it is $100,000/240 = $416.67 (rounded). Jot this number on a piece of paper.

B. Multiply the periodic interest rate by the principal. In our example, this is 0.0095833 x $100,000 = $958.33. Add this to the number arrived at in step A, and this gives you the first repayment for a reducing mortgage. In our example, this is $416.67 + $958.33 = $1,375.

The second payment will be slightly less than this. The third payment slightly less again, and so on.

C. Multiply the periodic interest rate by the number arrived at in step A. In our example, this is 0.0095833 x $416.67 = $3.99. Add this to the number arrived at in step A. In our case, $3.99 + $416.67 = $420.66. This gives you the final repayment for a reducing mortgage.

Flat mortgage

Multiply the periodic interest rate by the principal. This gives the repayment each month. In our example, this is 0.0095833 x $100,000 = $958.33.

At the end of the term, the principal is repaid.

6

VALUATIONS

A valuation forms an important part of buying, selling and owning property.

A valuation is an independent description of a property and its value. But don't rely on a valuer's report to give detailed analysis of a house's structure and potential problems. Most valuers aren't qualified builders or engineers and valuations aren't designed as an assessment of a property's structural soundness.

There are two types of valuations: private valuations which you can commission at any stage, and government valuations which are undertaken by Valuation New Zealand, a government agency. We look at each in turn, and then take a look at New Zealand house prices over the past fifteen years.

PRIVATE VALUATIONS

If you're thinking of hiring a valuer make sure the valuer is registered, a member of the New Zealand Institute of Valuers (PO Box 27-146 Wellington), and has a current Annual Practising Certificate. Anyone can call themselves a valuer, but a registered valuer must be professionally trained and must operate according to the NZIV's code of ethics and minimum standards. Shop around and make sure the valuers you contact are experienced in residential valuing.

There are a number of situations when it's useful to obtain a valuation of a property:

- If you're planning to buy the property. Mortgage lenders may require an up-to-date valuation of the property before they'll lend you the money.

- A valuation can also be useful if you're planning to sell your property. The valuation gives you a good indication of the price you should ask for your property. It might help to clinch a deal as well. You can mention to prospective buyers that you've got a recent valuation. The buyer's lender may accept this valuation, which means the buyer won't have to pay for one.
- When you're planning major home improvements. The valuation will tell you how the house's value will be affected by the planned improvements. You can compare this with the cost of the improvements.
- If your house is to be demolished for a public works scheme, a valuation can be a good independent assessment of the compensation you're entitled to. Also, if your marriage has failed, an independent valuation may be acceptable to both ex-partners.
- If you're disputing the government valuation (GV) of your property.

What you'll get

The valuation is in writing, and will detail:

- The value of the property, the purpose and date of the valuation.
- A description of the property, its address, ownership, zoning and size. The report may note any obvious structural flaws, but you shouldn't rely on it for this.
- The information the valuer has collected to help establish the valuation. You should receive the valuation within one or two weeks of the valuer's visit.

A valuation may not reflect the actual price a house sells for. The seller may be keen to sell, and so prices the house below its value. Nevertheless, valuations are generally a good indication of what the house should reasonably sell for. Different valuations of the same property undertaken at the same time and on the same basis shouldn't differ by more than five or 10 percent.

After you receive the valuation, call the valuer for a chat about the house and the area. You could pick up additional information not in the report, such as the valuer's opinion on future house price trends for the area.

Cost

House valuations undertaken by registered valuers usually cost between $200 and $500, depending on how difficult the property will be to value. Ask for a quote and shop around. When we surveyed the fees of five Wellington valuers a few years ago, we found a 35 percent variation in quotes for the same work. Some valuers offer a discount for cash or prompt payment.

To save money, you can ask for a "short report", which is a valuation with less detail available for a lesser fee. This may be sufficient in some cases, such as to establish a selling price, but probably won't satisfy a mortgage lender.

You can also get some estimated valuations, which are far cheaper. For less than $100, an Auckland-based firm, Val-Net, will provide a valuation of your home over the phone (the bill is charged to your telephone account). But of course Val-Net does not visit the property.

GOVERNMENT VALUATIONS

All real estate is usually valued every three years by Valuation New Zealand (VNZ), a government agency. These GVs are often used in calculating rates. VNZ will also produce a revised valuation in a number of cases (for example, if there is new building work undertaken on a property for which a building consent was issued).

VNZ produces three values for each property: the land value, the value of improvements (including any buildings, fences and swimming pools) and the capital value, which is the sum of the first two. The term "GV" usually refers to the capital value. Whenever your property is revalued, you are sent a notice of valuation detailing these three values.

A GV does not include the value of any chattels (such as floor coverings), nor does it take into account encumbrances on the property (these are legal claims on the property, like a mortgage) which can affect its market value.

Government valuers don't visit every property each time it is revalued. They do, however, inspect all properties for which building consents have been issued, or where new subdivisions have gone in. They also visit many properties that have sold. VNZ valuers have access to substantial amounts of data and may use computer models to estimate values (which are verified or altered as necessary through inspections of a sample of properties in each area).

If you disagree with any aspect of the notice of valuation, you have several weeks from the time you receive it to object. The details will accompany the notice.

Start by contacting your local VNZ office. Simple problems, such as your name has been misspelt, can easily be fixed. But you may dispute the actual valuation. This could happen, for example, when you believe that your house has been overvalued and therefore your rates will be too high.

If you do dispute the valuation, a government valuer will discuss your objection and possibly visit your property. During the period for hearing complaints, you can compare your valuation with the GVs and sale prices of comparable properties.

In light of your objection, VNZ may alter its valuation. If you remain dissatisfied, you can request that the matter be referred to the Land Valuation Tribunal. You must pay a fee for a hearing and produce tangible proof to support your claim (such as an independent valuation). You can appeal a tribunal decision to the High Court and the Court of Appeal.

Other VNZ services

VNZ offers a range of other services, particularly useful for house buyers:

- If you're planning a major move, say to a new city, go to your local library and consult VNZ's property statistics publications: Urban Property Sales Statistics and Rural Property Sales Statistics. These give useful information on average sale prices and turnover in the area.
- If you've got your eye on a particular place, ask the seller for the property's GV and its date. The GV gives you a guide to the property's value, but remember the GV excludes encumbrances and chattels.
- Also, if you're interested in a particular place, for a small fee you can obtain from VNZ the sales history of the property back to 1980. VNZ can also supply you with the sales histories of similar properties in the area. You can see from this whether they're selling above or below their GV. This gives you a good feeling for the market. Sellers can also use such information to help set their asking price.

REAL HOUSE PRICES

Is residential property a good investment? Of course, there's the intangible benefits of home ownership – security and the knowledge that any improvements that you make to the house are yours to keep.

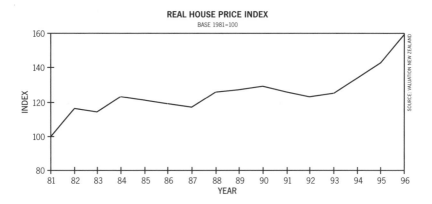

REAL HOUSE PRICE INDEX
BASE 1981=100

But the figures show that residential property can earn a good real return in hard dollars and cents as well. The graph shows the real (ie, adjusted for inflation) house price index from 1981 to 1996. It is based on figures published by VNZ, and shows that real house prices have boomed in the last few years. Indeed, while the real price rose 26 percent in the ten years to 1991, it rose by the same amount again from 1991 to 1996.

But real price rises are by no means guaranteed. In 1970s, for example, real house prices went on a roller coaster ride, rising throughout the first half of the decade and dropping away during the second half.

7

GETTING IT BUILT

Having a new house built can be very exciting, but there are risks. Build without council approval, or hire a shonky builder, and you're buying yourself a whole heap of trouble.

In this chapter we explain how to get the job done properly.

Having a house built is a six-stage process.

1. GET YOUR IDEAS TOGETHER

Decide what sort of house you want and can afford. The basic purpose of a house is to provide convenient and comfortable living conditions for the inhabitants. Exterior appearance is important, but the basic goal is a plan that gives good linking of all rooms with a minimum waste of floor area.

Identify your needs. How many bedrooms will you want? Do you intend to have children, or more children? Will they need separate bedrooms? What about study or play areas for the kids? Swimming pools? Patio? Will you need space for formal entertaining? Single or double garage? Room for hobbies? Extra storage space? Do you want a single- or multi-storey house? Will there be elderly or disabled people in the house? If so, what are their special needs?

To get some ideas, have a look at magazines, new subdivisions, open houses, books and talk to friends.

Once you've put together a very general picture of what you're after, you can contact the professionals. They should discuss your ideas with you and prepare sketch plans, which are used to obtain broad approval from the council for your plans. Once you have that approval, final plans and specifications can be drawn up and building consents (formerly known as building permits) obtained.

2. PLANNING

This are four main sources of building plans and specifications. Whichever expert you use, it's best to pick one who has professional indemnity insurance and/or guarantees their work.

Architect

This can be the most expensive option. Only around 10 percent of new houses are designed by architects. But if you can afford one, the architect can create a house that is uniquely yours and which perfectly suits the site.

An architect can advise you on the best location of the house, taking into account sunlight, view, winds and access. In some cases, such as for a sloping section or for retaining walls, an engineer's plans will also be needed. The architect may subcontract that part of the work or ask you to hire an engineer separately.

If you want, the architect can also handle all the work with the council, tender for builders, find a good section, supervise the construction, etc. This, of course, will cost you more. And although this is a useful service, you should also keep tabs on the building work yourself. It's your money at stake, after all.

To find a good architect, shop around. Ask each architect whether they have experience designing the sort of place you want. Once you've got a short list of two or three possibilities, discuss your plans with them and ask for an estimate of the fee. Ask for references and to see examples of houses they've designed (and to talk to the owners).

For a full service job (including designing your house, obtaining consents and supervising construction), an architect may charge a fee of seven to 12 percent of the construction cost. Check that any quote or estimate includes disbursements and GST. For a lesser fee, architects can sometimes provide 'off-the-shelf' plans which are adapted for your needs.

By law, anyone calling themselves an architect must be registered with the Architects Education and Registration Board and must have been professionally trained. Most belong to the New Zealand Institute of Architects (PO Box 438 Wellington), which requires its members to adhere to a code of ethics. A list of which architects belong is available from the NZIA.

Architectural designers

These are usually cheaper than architects and some offer very good service. Some architectural designers work for architects, others are self-employed.

But someone calling themselves an 'architectural designer' may or may not be professionally trained. This makes it even more important to make sure such a person has experience in designing homes. Ask for references, qualifications and check out previous examples of the designer's work.

There is a professional association of self-employed architectural designers: the Architectural Designers of New Zealand (PO Box 259 Tauranga). If you want to use a designer, we think it's worthwhile seeking out a member of this association to do the job. Members must have the New Zealand Certificate of Draughting (a polytechnic qualification) and at least three years' experience, or no qualification but five years' experience.

Builder

Some builders are competent at drawing up plans and can often adapt a basic layout to suit your requirements. Shop around and ask to see examples of the builder's work.

House building company

Here, you usually deal with sales staff who have a wide range of stock house designs and plans. For an additional fee, these plans can be adapted to suit your needs.

You and the expert (be it an architect, architectural designer or whatever) must sign a contract outlining what work is required and the agreed payment. Make sure you understand the document before signing. You may want to seek legal advice before signing, particularly if a lot of money is involved.

Once you've hired the expert, work with them on putting the plans together. If you're dissatisfied with any aspect of the developing plans, tell the expert. Ask for an explanation of anything you don't understand.

While you should feel free to change your mind, expect to pay extra if the expert has to alter the plans radically as a result of your change of heart.

3. COUNCIL APPROVAL

Under the Building Act, each local authority (city or district council) is responsible for administering the building code in its area. It has the power to make special dispensations for plans which vary from the code in a minor way.

Each authority issues building consents only for work which it is satisfied complies with the code.

It's your responsibility to obtain the required consents. If you go ahead and build without the proper consents, you may be fined and/or made to dismantle what's been built. You can, however, write into any contract that, say, the architect or the builder must obtain all appropriate council consents.

If you decide to get the consents yourself, begin by obtaining a copy of your property's certificate of title from Land Information New Zealand (LINZ, a government agency, previously known as the Department of Survey and Land Information or DOSLI). This document, which gives your property's legal description, is often the first requirement for obtaining any information from council.

You can obtain a project information memorandum. This will detail a lot of useful information. For more details, see our chapter on checking out houses.

Armed with your sketch plans, go along to the council to get a resource consent for what you intend doing. Check the council's district plan too. This can contain height restrictions, sunlight angles, restrictions on site coverage, etc., all of which could have an impact on your plans. Check, too, that there are no heritage restrictions on your property.

Assuming everything is in order, you can have the final plans drawn up. You return to the council with these and fill out an application form for a building consent. Generally, the Building Act requires councils to process a building consent application within 10 working days. This period can be extended as long as the council tells you why. If you haven't heard anything after two weeks, chase it up. If the council comes back to you seeking more information, the process starts all over again for another 10 working days.

The price of consents depends on the work involved. Expect to pay several hundred dollars.

The building consent will also detail a timetable for council building officers to visit your site to ensure the building work is complying with the approved plans. Don't proceed with building work until you're certain that the building officer is happy with it.

When the building job is finished, it's up to you to inform the council. The building officer will make a final visit and, if satisfied that everything is in order, will issue a code compliance certificate.

Keep the certificate. When you come to sell the place, it's proof that the job was done properly and to council standards. Also, if a building problem arises within 10 years of the certificate being issued, and you can prove that the problem was a result of the building officer's negligence, you can claim compensation.

Around the country there are a number of independent building certifiers who provide these services in competition with councils. They may charge you a lower fee.

4. CHOOSE A BUILDER

Once you've got the plans, specifications and the consents, you can start building. Shop around before hiring a builder. You should base your choice of builder on four criteria:

- Recommendations from the builder's previous clients. To find someone local who's good, talk to friends, neighbours, the architect, and workmates. You can also look through advertisements in local papers, the Yellow Pages, or contact the New Zealand Master Builders' Federation (PO Box 1796 Wellington).

  Builders who live in the area often rely on word of mouth for continuity of work. This means they're more likely to invest in their own future by doing a good job. You can also ask for references and inspect previous jobs the builder has completed.

- The builder's manner. House alterations can be a big hassle for you and your family. You need to feel that the builder is a reasonable sort of person, has a professional manner and is someone you'll get on with.

- Any guarantees available on the builder's work, such as a Master Build guarantee. We think it's wise to use a registered master builder and to obtain a guarantee, particularly if you're having a house built. Not all builders, however, are members of the federation and some non-members are very good. Whoever you choose as your builder, make sure you have a written, signed and dated contract.

- The builder's quote or estimate for the job. Get quotes from at least three builders. Give your written instructions to each of the builders and ask for a written quote that includes all costs and GST. Remember that a quote is a fixed price for a job, whereas an estimate is not.

  Each quote should contain a detailed list of all the work to be done. It should give separate costs for labour and materials. Ask, too, for the builder's hourly rate, in case any additional work is required later.

  Insist on a quote. If the quote is accepted, this will be the contract price. If you already know and trust a builder, you may want to negotiate a price solely with that builder. That's fine, but you should do this only if you have an idea of the going rate for the work. *Consumer* magazine regularly publishes trade rates.

Be wary of quotes that are a lot cheaper than the others, or of builders who'll quote for work that other builders say is too unpredictable. Ask them how they can charge so little, and point out any potential problem areas with the job. If you're satisfied that they know what they're doing, sign them up. But if you have any doubts, go elsewhere. A cheap price is little compensation for a poor job done by a builder who won't come back to fix up the mess.

Discuss materials with the builders. You may be able to source some materials yourself. Generally, though, builders can obtain materials at trade prices whereas you may have to pay retail.

Quotes usually apply only for a certain period. If you have delayed accepting a quote, make sure it's still current.

5. DRAW UP AND SIGN THE CONTRACT

Before agreeing to anything, draw up a contract for the job. A contract to have a house built must be a fully detailed document, checked (and possibly drawn up by) a lawyer. Our checklist at the end of this chapter gives the essentials that any building contract should cover.

Some organisations and builders have standard contracts available that you can use. Read any proposed contract carefully. In 1995, we had a look at the standard contracts on offer and found problems with them. For example, some had no clauses detailing start and finish dates; others were overly long and complicated.

Remember that any proposed contract is a starting position for negotiation. Make sure all the contract essentials noted in our checklist are covered. Strike out or alter any clauses which you don't like or which aren't relevant for your job, and add any others you think are important. Of course, the builder will have to agree to any changes.

With large jobs, builders usually require instalment payment as the work progresses. That's fine, but don't pay large amounts up front. We know of one case where a consumer paid the total cost of building materials before they were delivered. The amount was thousands of dollars. The goods didn't arrive and the consumer had to pay for replacement materials. After that, the first lot of goods did appear. He asked the supplier to take the goods back and give him a refund, but the supplier refused.

Here, the consumer would have a case under the Consumer Guarantees Act in that the service he received was unreasonable. Nevertheless, he'd have been better off not paying all the money in the first place.

Make sure the contract spells out what work will be completed by the dates that instalment payments are due. The contract should state that you'll inspect the work on those dates. If you're satisfied, the builder will be paid. If not, you can withhold payment until the work is up to scratch.

Building a house will require a variety of other tradespeople, including plumbers, plasterers and electricians. The contract should stipulate who'll be liable for subcontractors' mistakes. Most people hand the whole job over to the builder or architect, who is then responsible for the plumber, electrician and so on. That's usually a good idea. It means you have to deal directly with only one contractor.

If you have the time and are good at organising, you can save money by contracting and supervising everybody yourself. But remember, if something goes wrong it's up to you to sort it all out. You'll also be responsible to ensure all relevant legislation is complied with (such as the Employment Contracts and the Health and Safety in Employment Acts).

Standard contracts often include an escalation clause. This is a percentage margin (the exact amount is inserted into each contract) by which the contract price can be increased. This margin covers cost rises resulting from such things as materials, subcontractors or services increasing in price after the date of the quotation but before the building work is completed. The margin also covers work where the extent is unknown, for example, excavation.

We think a quote should be just that, a fixed price. In these days of low inflation we don't think that builders should be able to increase the price because material costs may rise. We do, however, accept that escalation clauses are sometimes unavoidable. In cases where additional work may be required, the contract should set an hourly rate for that part of the job.

Check that the contract covers insurance. On new buildings, contractors should have public liability insurance to cover their work. This covers any damage and other losses they cause. The builder should also have contract works insurance in the joint names of both the client and the builder. This will cover the construction. For example, it will cover your half-built house should it burn down.

The contract must set out the procedure for resolving disputes. These can be:

- Disputes Tribunal. At the time of writing, the cost is $10 for disputes up to $1,000, and $20 thereafter. You can take a case up to $3,000, or $5,000 if both parties agree. It's expected, however, that in 1997 the limits will rise to

$5,000, or $10,000 if both sides agree. If you're unclear what the limit is, contact the Department for Courts.

- Trade association. The Master Builders' Federation provides an inspection and complaints service for disputes over members' work. If you're hiring subcontractors yourself, a number of other trade associations (such as the Master Painters' Association and the Master Plumbers' Association) offer similar services. There may be a small fee which may be waived if your complaint is upheld.
- Arbitration. The Arbitrators and Mediators Institute of New Zealand (PO Box 1477 Wellington) can give you names of local arbitrators and mediators with relevant expertise.
- Court action. Use this only if it's absolutely necessary – it can be expensive and take years.

The contract should also require the builder to tidy up the site once the job is completed.

The contract should include a maintenance period. Usually this is 30 days from the date of completion but it may be as much as 90 days. If any problems arise during the maintenance period, the builder must remedy them. It is usual for the client to retain a percentage of the total price, say 10 percent, during this period. Assuming that everything is in order, this money is paid at the end of the maintenance period.

If you're in any doubt about an issue, discuss the matter with the builder.

Make sure both parties agree to the contract in writing – by signing and dating it – before the job starts.

6. MONITOR THE JOB

Keep an eye on the job as it goes along. Keep a diary of progress. Take photos and date them. Give all instructions to the builder in writing. If there are any serious changes of plan during construction, put these in writing and get both parties to sign and date the agreed changes and revised costs.

Give one copy of any written documentation to the builder and keep a copy yourself.

If you're unhappy with progress, tell the builder as soon as possible so that any problems can be sorted out. If you can't agree, make your concerns known to the builder in writing and keep copies of all correspondence. If you still can't agree, you'll have to initiate the dispute resolution proceedings set out in the contract.

Some materials, such as roof tiles or the stove, come with their own guarantees. Make sure you get these guarantees from the contractors. Many materials also have specific maintenance requirements (some of which must be followed for the guarantees to be valid), so make sure you receive all the relevant technical literature which accompany the materials.

Checklist of contract essentials

The following points should be covered in any building contract:

☐ Basic details
Your name and address, the address of the site and that of the builder.

☐ The contractor's obligations
- Complete all the work shown on the drawings and described in the specifications.
- Use good quality materials and workmanship.
- Comply with the Building Act and all other relevant laws and regulations.
- Pay all fees for the building consent, code compliance certificate and the like.
- Start and finish the work on the stated dates (subject to weather delays).
- Have public liability insurance and insure the work.
- Leave the site in a neat and tidy state.
- Make good faults and poor workmanship for at least 30 days (always try for a longer period and remember that, after this time, you have some protection under the Consumers Guarantees Act).
- Make good any damage caused by the contractor or subcontractors.
- Ensure that the site and tools used are safe, as required by the Health and Safety in Employment Act.

☐ Your obligations
- Pay the agreed price. This may be in stages. The contract should give a timetable setting out when payment is due, how much is due and what work must be completed before payment is made.
- Give the contractor reasonable access to the site.
- Give the contractor all relevant details about the work and the site.
- You may also agree to provide secure storage for the contractor.

☐ Variations

This is the term for any changes you agree to make to the plan or specifications after the contract is signed. Variations must be costed and agreed to in writing between you and the contractor.

☐ Standards

If, in the opinion of a stipulated independent expert (such as the Master Builder's Federation), the work is not of an acceptable standard, you may terminate the contract and pay only the value of the work done. Also, you have the right to deduct any additional costs involved in getting others to finish the work.

☐ Final payment

Final payment (say, 10 percent of the total) should not be made until all work is completed and the site is cleared and made good as required by the contract.

☐ Late payment

If you don't pay on time for work that has been competently done, the contractor may terminate the contract and claim the outstanding payment from you.

☐ Disputes

If there's a dispute between you and the contractor, neither side can terminate the contract until it has been heard by a stipulated independent arbitrator or, if the value of the matter in dispute is within the appropriate limits, the Disputes Tribunal.

8

HOME IMPROVEMENTS AS AN INVESTMENT

One of the joys of owning your own home is having control over your environment. You can pick wallpapers and paint colours to suit your own taste, and gradually alter the place to fit your lifestyle. Once you've done essential renovations, anything extra is an indulgence – just like spending a big sum at a resort in Fiji or Bali, or buying the latest home theatre system.

But we often renovate with the expectation that we're making an investment. We hope the work will improve the property value by at least the amount of the cost and, we hope, more. That's where this chapter can help. We provide tips on jobs you can do which really will be an investment in your home, and warn you away from some costly mistakes.

But before you get out the dustsheets, work out whether it's better to improve or move. If you're going to spend big money on a house which you may not get back, then think about shifting. Want to live in a low-maintenance, contemporary style home? You'd almost always do best to buy one. Don't try to turn a Californian bungalow or Edwardian villa into a modern house.

Depending on the value of your home, how you sell and how you shift, moving house could easily cost you $10,000 if you include a real estate agent's commission, so it's not something you'd do lightly. But if, after doing the costing and getting estimates of the value after improvements, renovations are likely to cost more than $10,000 above the likely rise in value, then you're better to shift.

HOW TO CALCULATE THE COSTS

The rest of the chapter assumes that you're considering only work that could increase the property value at least to cover the cost of the job. The biggest risk here is overcapitalising: pouring money into your home which you wouldn't get back if you were to sell. The financial risk here is worsened if you borrow to do the job, because then you're making interest payments on the loan in addition to the construction costs.

If you're thinking in investment terms, you also have to consider inflation. Let's say that you bought the house for $150,000 in June 1991. Since then, you've spent $15,000 on renovations. The house valuation in June 1996 was $178,000. So your renovations paid off, right?

Not necessarily. Just to keep pace with inflation, your house value would have had to rise to $165,450 over that time. So you've received a gain after inflation of just $12,550. There's a shortfall here from what you spent.

So how can you reduce the risks of overcapitalising? First, get an estimate of the total cost of the job. This will be based on quotes from tradespeople, local authority consent costs (if necessary), will include GST and will also allow an extra 10 percent on top for the unexpected.

Then go for expert advice. For an informal estimate of the impact on value of the work you're planning, you could talk to a real estate agent who specialises in your area. What type of facilities do people expect in your neighbourhood? Are you planning something which buyers are clamouring for? Or would your renovations put your house above all others in the suburb, making it difficult to get your money back?

You could pay for a registered valuation, with estimates of the market value of your house before and after the intended renovations. This is likely to cost around $250 to $400, depending on where you live and the company you contact, but for major renovations it's a good step to take.

A key guideline is to spend according to the value of the house. For example, don't put a $40,000 kitchen into a $120,000 house. It's a good rule of thumb that you shouldn't spend more than 10 percent of your house's total value on a new kitchen.

The most cost-effective renovation work is that done on bad houses in good streets. You can lift the value of a house closer to that of its neighbours. But if you take the top house in a poor street, the fact that surrounding houses all cost less will limit potential rises in value.

RENOVATING TO SELL OR TO KEEP

"First impression" is the key phrase to bear in mind if you're planning to renovate before selling your house. It's the first few minutes in the house that will attract buyers, or turn them off. So appearance is the key. If paintwork is flaking, then get out your paintbrush.

Replacing faded curtains can cost the earth, but if you shop carefully you should be able to find some new ones that look good but won't have a huge price tag.

Work out how much it will cost to replace anything that looks particularly worn or soiled. For instance, you may find that you can replace scratched kitchen lino with new for a few hundred dollars, giving the whole room a fresher and brighter feel.

Bear in mind that the garden is also important in establishing a first impression. If the front door is darkened by a tangled forest of unkempt shrubs, trim them right back, or pull them out and replace them. An easy care, colourful and attractive garden will enhance the appearance of the property.

If you're planning to stay in the house a long time, the rules are different. Before you pull out colour charts and carry wallpaper books home, you need to get the framework of the house right. This means working out the layout of rooms you want and, if necessary, repiling, relevelling and rewiring, before you give any thought to decoration.

The positives

Anything that makes dark areas lighter, does away with clutter, reduces the need for maintenance or increases convenience is likely to add value. Exactly how much in dollar terms depends on your house value, neighbourhood and region. But worth considering in all parts of the country are:

- Redecorating and adding simple fittings
  Paint in light, popular shades. Get rid of dark colours and replace flowery expanses of 1970s wallpaper. Put heated towel rails in the bathroom and perhaps a shaver point.
- New lights and skylights
  Good lighting in kitchens and bathrooms is essential, and the choice of light fittings is vast. As with our kitchen lino example, spending just a few hundred dollars can transform the "feel" of a room, making it bright and welcoming.

  Nothing can quite replace the effect of natural light, however, and skylights are worth investigating as a solution to a gloomy kitchen or hallway.

The cheapest type have a dome above the roof, which collects lights and passes it down a reflective flexible tube into the room; these can cost well under $1,000 installed, depending on the brand, the construction of your home and the space between ceiling and roof.

Larger skylights built from timber and glass can completely open up a room, making it feel bigger and more attractive.

- Easy clean, work-friendly kitchen

  If you're planning a kitchen renovation, think about cleaning and work layout. One decision you'll have to make, for example, is whether to have a free-standing stove, or a wall or underbench oven and a cooktop built into a benchtop. Free-standing stoves have the disadvantage that food scraps can spill into the narrow gap at either side of the stove, a difficult place to clean.

  The layout of the kitchen should be logical. The placement of ovens, fridges, the height of worktops and so on is almost a science in itself. A kitchen designer will be able to give you good advice, or you can look through books on kitchen design at your library.

  Make sure there's plenty of well-lit benchspace and good storage. In new cabinetry, allow space for a microwave and dishwasher, and a vented range-hood over the cooktop.

- Extra space

  In general, building another room or extending a boxy little space into a comfortable living room will increase a property's value. If you have an older home with a large attic space, converting some of this to a bedroom may be worthwhile, particularly if there's a pleasant outlook from this height.

  But if you're doing major rebuilding, think first about function and what buyers might expect. If your addition is a new master bedroom to a house in an expensive area, would potential buyers in that area expect it to have an en suite, or a walk-in wardrobe? If you're adding a new living area, make sure it will fit comfortably with the "flow" of the house, or will create an improved flow.

  A cheaper option could be to add a wooden deck with access through french doors. If you have a suitably sunny and sheltered location, then you have what can be used as an extra room in fine weather.

  Think also about the potential of your garage or workshop. Properly lined, this could offer useful storage.

The negatives

As we've mentioned before, particular renovations will have a different impact on your value, depending on the house's value to start with, the general level of house values in your area and what part of the country you live in. But there are some types of work which real estate agents and valuers from different parts of the country all agree may not be worth doing. In some cases, these renovations can put off potential buyers, and even lower the value of your property. Here are the most common things you shouldn't do:

- Anything unusual
We've heard about amateur astronomers constructing observatories in their back yards, and movie buffs building windowless rooms for screening. If you're planning to stay in your home long term, changes to accommodate specific hobbies can add a great deal to your lifestyle. But unless your favourite leisure activity is one shared by most of the population, altering your house in this way won't add to the value of your property.

- Work out of character
Sanding down the wooden sash windows in a Victorian villa isn't the best way to spend summer weekends, but don't be tempted to replace the kauri or rimu with aluminium windows, or to rip out the original tiled fireplaces and replace them with a modern heater. There's a strong demand for character. Destroy that character, and you'll put off a lot of potential buyers. Instead, look at other options. If you don't like the hassle of an open fire, can you find a gas fire that can be installed in the original fireplace?

It's possible to add modern conveniences to an Edwardian villa or Art Deco bungalow, but such changes should be done sensitively and should complement the original style.

This also applies to grounds and outbuildings. If your Victorian villa is surrounded by an attractive cottage garden, when it comes to replacing a dilapidated garage, opt for a style which won't clash with your property's character.

- Improvements requiring ongoing maintenance
Swimming pools, for example, require regular cleaning. If you put in a water-heating system, the costs of that, on top of the maintenance of the pool, could discourage many buyers. Do something like this only if you're planning to stay a long time.

- Anything that reduces important areas
If, for instance, you brick up the garage door to create a games room or spa room, or you knock down a wall and turn 2 bedrooms into one, this could easily reduce the value of your home.

- Botched or unfinished jobs
It may be better to keep something in its original state, rather than leaving

bristles and brushmarks in hasty paintwork, mismatched wallpaper or incomplete renovations. We've even seen one house where the wallpaper was put up so hastily, that the pattern was upside down!

Whatever you do, make sure that you get any consents which may be necessary, and, for major work, a code compliance certificate (CCC) from your council. Even after you've sold the property, legal action can be brought against you for negligent work done without the right consents.

You should also stick to well-qualified tradespeople. After major electrical work, ask your electrician for a certificate of compliance.

9

BUYING FOR INVESTMENT

There's something about property that's dear to the New Zealand heart. Not only is owning your own house an almost universal aspiration, but many people go on to buy a rental property as well. When the Retirement Commissioner surveyed the ways people save for their retirement, he found that rental property was one of the most popular investments.

In recent years, this type of investment has faced a challenge. Independent financial advisers will tell you to spread your investments around, in shares and fixed interest as well as property. Plunging your spare cash into a rental property, when you already own the house you live in, is, they say, putting all your eggs in one basket.

In 1991, for example, the average house sale price fell in New Zealand. Yet that year was a strong one for the sharemarket, with many unit trusts invested in shares giving returns over 20 percent.

Others will point out that the huge property price rises of the past relied heavily on inflation. They say that the Reserve Bank's inflation crackdown will dampen likely rises in future.

ADVANTAGES AND DISADVANTAGES OF BUYING PROPERTY

So how does buying property stack up as an investment? There's no long-term residential property index which includes both income and price changes, as the NZSE 40 does for shares. But there is an index run by Valuation New Zealand which looks at freehold open market sales.

We combined these figures with inflation (consumer price index) figures from Statistics New Zealand, and found good news for residential property investors.

During the five years to 30 June 1996, the index rose by an average 4.72 percent per year after inflation; in the last 10 years, 2.89 percent; the last 20 years, 0.72 percent per year. Remember that's just a capital gain, with income to come on top.

The high growth of the past five years will be at least partly due to Auckland's boom, and won't necessarily be true for other centres. But it shows that, despite what some pundits say, residential property can provide good gains even in a low-inflation environment.

Prices are likely to continue upward, driven by population increase, relative prosperity for many people, easy access to mortgage finance, and an economic outlook which gives people the confidence to make long-term commitments.

Values don't go upwards in a continuous smooth line. In fact, the overall average residential property price index has fallen in real terms on more than one occasion over the past fifteen years (see table page 43). In some parts of the United States, property prices have fallen for a decade. And the averages are just that – averages over the whole country. The prices in different regions, and different locations within regions, will perform at different rates.

Having most of your investment dollars tied up in property is taking a risk, and where you buy will be crucial. But if you buy in growing areas, it's likely that, in the long term, residential property prices will continue to grow by around one to three percent per annum after inflation.

There are other advantages and disadvantages you need to consider:

Advantages

- Capital gains can be substantial and, if you don't buy for the purpose of resale, aren't taxed.
- It's a way to build a substantial investment while holding down a fulltime job elsewhere.
- You have hands-on control of your own investment.
- It's a way of buying an expensive asset for a deposit of only a quarter of the price or less.
- There are substantial tax deductions available.

Disadvantages

- Property prices go up and down. You can lose out if you're forced to sell during a down period.

- There are swings in the rental market. A glut of rental buildings, or a shortage of tenants, may force rents down.
- It's not an investment you can cash up quickly. When it comes to selling you may have to wait months to find a buyer.
- If the expenses on the property are greater than the income from it, then you have to put money from other income – such as a salary or wages – into the property, and that won't suit everyone.
- You run the risk of having bad tenants who may damage the property or not pay rent.
- You have ongoing maintenance costs and inconvenience.
- Which location you choose to buy in is a crucial decision and requires careful research.

THE FINANCES

You may be surprised to find that this section, on financing an investment property, is much longer than the subsequent section about selecting a property and tenants. But the financial area, more than any other, is where most people come to grief. Understanding the financial side is the key to success in property investment.

Your budget

Before you start looking for a house or a flat, you need to collect some information together and work out a rough budget. This will guide you in what you can afford, whether you will get a net return from the investment, or whether you'll need to put money in. You must work out the likely income and expenses for a year.

On the income side there's only one figure that counts – the rent – but getting it right can prove tricky. First, work out roughly the type of property you can afford and where you can buy. Then, by looking through the newspaper flats/houses to let column, or by talking to letting agents, you can get an idea of the type of rent you can expect. It's best to be conservative here. Don't assume you'll get the top rent for a certain type of property: go for a figure in the middle. And to allow for turnover of tenants, don't expect to collect rents for 52 weeks a year: base your calculation on just 48 weeks' rent or, at the most, 50 weeks.

Next, you need to work out expenses. From your rough idea of the value of property you can afford, and where you'll buy, you'll have enough information to get an estimate of how much you'll pay in local authority rates and insurance. Your loan repayments will depend on how much you need to borrow. You can work out the loan repayments for a given amount of borrowing by using our guide at the end of Chapter 5.

Maintenance and repair costs depend largely on the property you buy, but again you should be reasonably conservative. We think $300 per year is the absolute minimum figure for this type of budget – many properties will cost more. Also add the likely legal fees, valuation and mortgage costs when you buy the property.

Now comes the analysis. Unless you're able to buy without a large loan, you'll commonly find that the expenses are more than the rental income, especially in the early years, and while mortgage interest rates are comparatively high. If you go ahead, you'll need to put money into the property from another source, such as your own salary or wages.

This doesn't mean that property is a dud investment: as we explain below, it can work out well if you expect property values to rise in the long term, and you're looking for capital gain rather than immediate income.

But just as you allow some margins in your figure calculations, also be conservative with your analysis. Allow for the possibility of interest rate rises, and bear in mind that you can't always bump up rent to cover them. What would happen in the worst case scenario, where the mortgage costs jumped and you had trouble finding tenants? Could you keep the payments up for a month or so?

Look at how much you'll need to put in from other sources, since this is one of the riskiest areas of the investment. If it takes big portions of your own income to service the loan, and you lose your job, or you're disabled for a period, then you could lose the property. If you have no paid sick or annual leave – you're self employed, for example, – consider income replacement insurance.

Raising the finance

Banks and other lenders generally regard rental properties slightly differently from owner-occupied homes. You're likely to need a larger deposit: many banks lend only up to 75 percent of a rental property's value.

When it comes to servicing a loan, they prefer to lend an amount where the repayments won't go much above 30 percent of your own gross salary or wages and 75 percent of the gross rental you expect.

If you have a written budget with conservative figures, you know what your cash flow will be and you know exactly how much you're asking for and what proportion of your income this is likely to be, all this information will make a very favourable impression on a banker or other lender.

Raising finance is quite easy if you've been in your own home for a few years. You could use the balance of available equity in your own home as a deposit to buy a second property which itself carries a mortgage. You should, however, understand the risk involved in this. A lower risk option is to put all your spare cash into paying off the mortgage on your own home, then saving for the deposit on a rental property.

The higher your debt (the higher you are "geared", as the jargon goes) the higher the potential gain or loss on a property. For example, say two people each buy a house for $150,000. One borrows 50 percent of the purchase price, the other borrows 75 percent. For the sake of simplicity, let's say they have interest-only mortgages.

If the values rise to $200,000 after two years, then the purchaser who borrowed less has seen his equity grow from $75,000 to $125,000 – or 67 percent. But the person who borrowed more has seen her equity rise from $37,500 to $87,500 – a jump of 133 percent!

But if the values fall to $125,000, the purchaser who borrowed less has seen his equity fall to two-thirds of its original amount; the purchaser who borrowed more has seen hers fall to just a third of its original value.

Gearing is generally used to allow a buyer to get into a higher value property than would otherwise be possible, or to buy more properties over time.

If the property needs upgrading, try to get a mortgage that allows you to make lower repayments in the first few months, so you can spend money on renovation. This is likely to work best if you've bought a run-down house in a very good area. By renovating it up to the standard of surrounding homes, you'll be able to attract good tenants and charge a higher rental than you could in poorer parts of town.

Make sure you have other credit available, but use it sparingly. Credit cards with limits of several thousand dollars will be useful to pay for unexpected and expensive repairs, for example, but in normal usage, pay off the full amount each month. You may find it convenient to take a mortgage which allows you to redraw some of the principal you've paid off.

However much you borrow, negotiate hard to get the best deal. For example, fees are generally negotiable. You may pay one percent of the total amount of the loan, or you may pay nothing. Don't be afraid to walk away from a finance deal that isn't completely right, just as you should walk away from a property that doesn't meet your needs.

The tax situation

To maximise the benefits of your property investment, it's crucial to claim the tax deductions available to you. It's possible to do your return yourself, but most landlords use accountants. This isn't necessarily expensive – simple returns can be prepared for $150 to $300, depending on the work needed and how tidy and complete your records are. But accountants can find all allowable deductions and they know recent cases and what guidelines the Inland Revenue Department (IRD) has released.

You have to pay income tax only on that portion of your income left after deducting all your legitimate tax expenses incurred in renting the property. You pay tax on your profit, not your revenue.

You can deduct against your rental income:
• Interest on money borrowed to buy the property
• Repairs, though only where you maintain the property to a certain standard, without improving it
• The cost of finding tenants (e.g. newspaper advertising)
• Building insurance and contents insurance for your chattels in the flat
• Local authority rates
• Accountancy fees
• Bank charges
• Cleaning when tenants have left, and property maintenance such as fortnightly lawnmowing
• Car expenses involved in your renting business
• Office expenses (e.g. if you have a small room in your home which you use as an office to conduct your property business, you can deduct the room's share of your home's costs such as mortgage interest, rates, insurance etc.)
• Depreciation on the property and chattels. This deduction is particularly valuable for two reasons. First, it can be quite large. Second, unlike the other deductions, it isn't based on hard cash which you've had to pay out during the year.

Building depreciation can be up to three or four percent per year, depending on the method used. It applies to any property you've bought to rent out, regardless of age. Buy a 100-year-old house as a rental property, and it can still be depreciated. Depreciation on carpets, curtains, stoves and other chattels is generally much higher. Tables of figures can be obtained from Inland Revenue.

Interest on a mortgage on your own home is deductible if you've borrowed the money to buy investment property. Understanding this is crucial: it's not which property is mortgaged that's important, but for what purpose you're using the borrowed funds.

Say you want to rent out the home you're currently living in, and move to a better place. You won't be able to claim interest as a tax deduction if you borrow money against either your existing or the new property to buy the new property, since it's not being bought as an investment.

The solution? Sell your existing house, and use this money to buy your new home. Then take out another loan to buy an investment property. This way, the interest is deductible.

If your deductions are larger than your income – as they often are in the early years, when you're usually paying the most interest on your loan – you incur no tax at all. Losses are written off against any tax you've paid elsewhere – they are deducted from other taxable income such as salary and wages and may reduce other taxable income to zero or a negative amount. The negative amount can be carried forward and offset against a future year's taxable income, or you could get a refund.

Say you have a fulltime job, paying PAYE tax, and you buy a rental property. If you make a loss on your property, this reduces your overall income. You can claim a refund on the PAYE income tax you paid on the income of your fulltime job.

Take this example, based on the tax scales as of 1 September 1996. You buy a property for $150,000, with a $37,500 deposit (from the equity in your own property). The mortgage interest rate is 10 percent, and the property is rented for $245 per week.

Because you're paying a high interest bill in the early days, this, on top of the other costs, means that the property is making a loss. It's costing you more than the $12,740 yearly rental income to keep it going. Let's say the tax-deductible costs of the property are $17,750 in the first year. You've made a loss on your rental business of $5,010. You can use that loss to offset the tax on your salary.

If your salary is $40,000, then you'd normally pay $9,267 in tax. But if you apply the figure above, the loss from the property means your total income falls to $34,990. So the total tax you pay will be only $8,143. You'll get a refund on the tax you've already paid through PAYE.

If a couple is buying an investment property for long-term gain, it should be bought in the name of the person on the higher taxable income, since they'll be able to make the best use of deductions. If a couple buys for income, the property should be bought in the name of the lower earning partner.

If there's a chance you may want to transfer ownership of rental property to other family members, it's worth discussing other ownership possibilities with your lawyer. You could set up a company to own property, for example. Although this involves a set-up cost, a separate tax return and an annual return to the Justice Department, it has the advantage of allowing the underlying ownership of the property to change hands through the transfer of shares: you don't need to go through the physical transfer of property title ownership.

Property can also be owned by a family trust. Talk to your lawyer to see which type of ownership best meets your needs.

Why on earth would you want to buy an investment which costs you money, leaving you with a lower income? The key reason is capital gain. You expect the property value to rise in the long term. But another advantage of property investment is that you claim, as tax deductions, costs you would have incurred anyway.

At the time of writing, there's no capital gains tax in New Zealand, although if you buy and sell regularly, or buy for the specific purpose of selling at a profit (as opposed to buying for the income or the long-term appreciation), the IRD may consider that you're in the business of dealing in houses, and thus charge tax on gains as though they were income.

Don't get hooked on tax deductions. It's nice getting a refund from Inland Revenue, but that's all it is – a refund on tax you've already paid. It's not a gift. Remember, in any investment, the thing to keep your eye on is the return after tax. We've heard some people say that they're not repaying a loan faster than they could because they'd lose the deductibility. But they've lost sight of the fact that the interest they're paying is far greater than the value of the deduction they can claim against the IRD. In other words, they're paying tens of thousands more just to get a few thousand back.

The only reason to remain in debt longer than you need to – remaining "geared" – is if there's an extremely high chance of capital gain that will leave you with a higher return after interest and tax are considered.

Living in your own investment

Many people who buy rental property will be buying a separate building from their own home, but that isn't always the case. You may buy a house which has a self-contained flat attached; you may buy a multi-flat property and live in one flat yourself; you may have a large home that you share with boarders or flatmates. You can still regard these as investments.

If you have just one flatmate or boarder in your home, it's a simple business. You keep all the rent. You're not required to mention this on your tax return, nor can you claim expenses. The Commissioner of Inland Revenue, for pragmatic reasons, treats the income as nil.

If you have two, three or four flatmates, there are two options open to you:

1. Declare 20 percent of the rent money in your tax return. You can't claim expenses, as that 20 percent is regarded as profit.

2. Declare all the income and claim for an appropriate proportion of expenses. Let's say there are three of you in a house, you and two flatmates. You claim two-thirds of available deductions. (If you have three flatmates, you would claim three-quarters of the deductions).

The second option requires more careful record-keeping and paperwork, and it's more work when it comes to doing your tax return. But it's the better choice if you think your profit is less than 20 percent of the income. It'll almost certainly be the better choice if you're paying off a big mortgage on the property.

This same principle is used if you live in one unit in a multi-unit property you've bought. Say you've bought a house that's been divided into two flats. You've rented out the other flat. In your tax return, you declare the income you get from the rent, and half the expenses of the total property.

Another option is to keep a record of the expenses that relate just to the part of the property you're renting out, and claim these against the income.

Negative gearing is also possible where you have boarders, flatmates or shared buildings.

The IRD has a free, easy-to-read booklet, Rental Income, which guides you through the tax issues involved in rental property. We recommend you read it.

THE PROPERTY AND THE TENANTS

What and how to buy

The potential for capital gain, and for getting and holding good tenants, is set on the day you buy the property, in particular by the location you've chosen, and the nature of the property itself. Look for something that's handy to public transport, shops, schools and other facilities.

Go looking in the best area you can afford, where people will be more keen to live, and be more likely to pay a higher level of rent. For the purpose of capital gain, consider which parts of town are likely to remain popular, and which may appreciate in value. As property values rise, rent levels rise.

Choose an area you're familiar with – you'll know the type of tenant looking for accommodation in that suburb, the rent levels you can ask and so on.

Be cautious about buying in an area where most of the jobs are provided by a single employer. If that business decides to close down or shift, the demand for rental properties could collapse.

By contrast, you're likely to find good demand from tenants if you buy within 20 minutes' walking distance of a university, polytechnic or city centre.

When it comes to considering a particular building, all the property checks outlined in Chapter 2 – getting a LIM from the local authority, building checks and so on – apply here.

Don't worry if a house has a few rooms that need repainting, or if the garden is scruffy: that's not expensive to put right. But it shouldn't require expensive structural work. For example, your personal taste may be for a romantic Edwardian villa surrounded by a cottage garden. But unless you're happy to spend all your weekends on home maintenance and gardening, you're better off to get a more recent building in permanent materials with a low-maintenance garden.

Don't buy anything with features that require a high level of ongoing maintenance, such as a swimming pool or spa pool. If you hope to attract a family as tenants, fill in fish ponds that could be deathtraps for toddlers. Look for fences, good carpets and curtains.

Remember that you're not buying a place to live in yourself. So you'll need to be much harder headed about your purchase. Make a low offer and negotiate hard. If you don't think you're getting a good deal, then walk away. A better deal will come up.

Tenants

Tenants are your customers. Welcoming them and keeping the good ones is important to your success.

It's better to undercut market rents slightly and hold good tenants for the long term, than try to get every last cent possible and then face the inconvenience and costs of a high turnover of tenants. But try to keep an eye on what's happening with rent levels, and don't be afraid to raise the rent if the market level has risen strongly.

When you're considering tenants, ask to see a reference from an employer or previous landlord. Judge people on such aspects as tidiness, cleanliness and ability to pay, rather than on any prejudices you may have against unmarried couples or children. You should also be aware of the provisions of the Human Rights Act in this area.

Treat your tenants well. It may help encourage them to look after your property if it's sparkling clean and tidy when they first move in. Oil squeaky doors, spray dry lubricant on sticking drawers. Get your tenants on side by leaving a bunch of flowers or a bottle of wine and a welcome card for their arrival. It's not an expensive gesture and it can make a good impression.

Most investment homes are let unfurnished. It reduces the damage that can be done to your property, and encourages stability of tenants: people are less likely to move out on a whim if it means arranging for all their furniture to be shifted as well.

Leave a sheet with the details of what day rubbish/recycling is collected, whether and when there are milk deliveries, when the buses run, where the closest post box is and any other useful information about the neighbourhood. Make your tenants feel welcome and get off on the right foot.

It's wise to go through the property with your tenant at the start and record what's there and the condition of the property and chattels. Tenancy Services, part of the Ministry of Housing, produce a tenancy agreement which includes a property inspection report that you can use.

Regardless of their keen promises when they first move in, you should assume that tenants will do no work on the property. It isn't expensive to get a lawnmowing service to trim the grass each fortnight.

The rights and responsibilities of landlords and tenants are spelt out in the Residential Tenancies Act 1986, the Residential Tenancies Amendment Act 1992 and the Residential Tenancies Amendment Act 1996. Key parts of those laws:

- You must have a written tenancy agreement for all tenancies entered into after 1 December 1996. Tenancy agreement forms are produced by Tenancy Services at the Ministry of Housing. For tenancies that began before this date, either party can require the agreement to be put in writing. You can't put in the agreement anything that conflicts with the Residential Tenancies Act. If you do, the Residential Tenancies Act provides that those terms will be unenforceable against the tenant.

- You can charge no more than four weeks' rent as a bond. This must be deposited with the Tenancy Services Bond Centre in Porirua within 23 working days of you receiving it. Where rent is paid up and there's been no damage to the rental property, this goes back to the tenants when they leave. But if damage has been done or there's rent owing, the landlord may get all or some of the bond.

- You can't charge rent more than two weeks in advance. Where rent is paid by cash or open cheque, you must provide a receipt.

- Rent increases cannot be less than six months apart and can be made only after 60 days' notice has been given.

- If you want to inspect the property or work done on the property by the tenant, you must give at least 48 hours' notice and not more than 14 days' notice. You can't make an inspection of the property more often than once every four weeks, and it must be between the hours of 8 a.m. and 7 p.m. If you want to enter the property to make repairs you must give at least 24 hours notice, and it must be between the hours of 8am and 7pm. Of course, you can enter at any time with the consent of the tenant, or if there's an emergency.

- Where there's no fixed term to the tenancy, a tenant wishing to end the tenancy must give 21 days' written notice, unless the landlord agrees in writing to a shorter time. A landlord must usually give 90 days' written notice, but this may be reduced to 42 days if the property is needed for the landlord or the landlord's family to move into, or the property has been sold with vacant possession, or if it's employee accommodation and is needed again for that purpose. Where the tenancy is a service tenancy, the landlord is required to give a minimum of two weeks' notice before termination.

- If your tenants have given notice and you want to show potential new tenants through, you can do that at any time with agreement of the existing tenants. Tenants consent cannot be unreasonably withheld, but they are able to put reasonable conditions on their consent.

- If you're planning to sell your rental property, you must notify the tenant of this in writing. You are also required to tell prospective tenants. As with potential new tenants, potential buyers can be shown through at any time with the agreement of the tenants. Again tenants consent cannot be unreasonably withheld but they are able to put reasonable conditions on their consent.

  After the sale, you have to give your tenants written details about the new owner's name and address.

- Some buyers will want to buy your property with vacant possession – i.e. no tenants. Make sure that you have sufficient time to give your tenants notice. Only agree on a settlement date which is comfortably after this time.

- If you have a tenant/landlord dispute, there are two kinds of help you can get from Tenancy Services. First, both parties could meet with a mediator and try to reach agreement. If an agreement is made, it's put in writing and can be legally binding. If you can't reach agreement, the Tenancy Tribunal can hear the dispute. The adjudicator's decision is final and legally binding.

  Tenancy Services also offers free advice to both landlords and tenants with regard to tenancy problems.

The Tribunal can end a tenancy if the rent is 21 days or more overdue; if you or the tenant's neighbours have been assaulted or threatened with assault; if the tenant has substantially damaged or threatened to damage the property, or abandoned the property; or if either party has made a written request for a breach to be remedied within 10 working days and this hasn't been done.

You should also be aware of the Human Rights Act. Under this legislation you can't refuse to let a place to someone on the basis of their race, colour, religious or ethical beliefs, marital status, sex or sexual orientation, or because they're pregnant, unemployed or have children.

The Residential Tenancies Act also prohibits you from discriminating against anyone on these grounds when you're considering new tenants, or whether to extend or alter an existing tenancy. And you can't ask a letting agent or property manager to discriminate for you.

Additional help

If you just have one or a couple of rental properties, you'll probably manage them yourself. But if you're prepared to pay someone else to do this, or you have a number of properties, you may wish to consider a professional manager.

Managers can help to find tenants, collect rent, arrange for repairs and maintenance, inspect the property regularly and carry out the other tasks you'd normally do yourself. For this their total costs are usually between seven and 10 percent of gross rents. On top of that, of course, you'll pay the charges of the tradespeople they engage to do any work on the property.

We've heard from some investors who've been very pleased with the peace of mind they get from good managers, and others who've been very unhappy with shoddy service. We recommend you ask around – perhaps among members of your local property investors' association – to see who has a good name in your area. And pay close attention to what is set out in the contract.

Letting agents simply find tenants for property. Their fee is paid by the tenant, not the landlord.

Local property investors' associations provide advice and support. Other owners may have contact details for good tradespeople or professional advisers, and be happy to share their experiences. There are 14 autonomous associations, which are members of the national federation. Membership nationwide is just under 2000. They offer publications, meetings, seminars and, in some cases, discount privileges.

10

HOLIDAY HOMES, TIMESHARES AND RETIREMENT VILLAGES

Much of the advice we give elsewhere in this book also applies to holiday homes and to apartments in retirement villages. But there are some unique tips and traps to watch out for in these properties. And, although timeshares should be seen more as holiday purchases than as real estate investments, the large sums of money involved mean it pays to know your rights under law.

HOLIDAY HOMES

"Twenty footprints to the sea. Cleared 1030m^2 Golden Bay beachfront section. Fantastic views of the bay. Scallops are fat. Think about your retirement..."

When the sun's baking the sand and the air's thick with the hum of summer insects, a holiday home seems like a great investment. For a few years, it could be somewhere to relax during leave from your job and over long weekends. Eventually, perhaps, you could build a more comfortable place to spend time when work is behind you.

In the most popular resorts, the prices involved will quickly shatter your dream. At prime waterfront locations in Northland, Taupo, the Marlborough Sounds and Queenstown, holiday homes can go for half a million dollars or more.

But move away from the big money places, and sections in pleasant spots can still be found for as little as $30,000, keeping the dream alive. You can have the shell of a small cottage erected on the site to lock-up stage for around $35,000. Put in some finishing and decorating work yourself, and you could have a holiday home in the sun for less than $80,000.

Homework

When you're examining the finances for a holiday home, you need to consider two things: first, look at the costs you'll face in the early years of ownership and, second, work out the capital gain potential.

A holiday home won't save you money on future holidays; holidays could even be twice as expensive. Let's take as an example an $80,000 bach. For simplicity, we've assumed an interest-only mortgage:

Interest on: $40,000 borrowed at 11% over 15 years	$4,400
Foregone tax-paid interest on $40,000 (what your deposit could earn if invested elsewhere, assume 5% net)	2,000
Maintenance and repairs	300
Insurance	300
Rates	400
Electricity supply	300
Total for year	$7,700

If your bach were used for eight weeks a year, holidays there are effectively costing you $962.50 per week. That's more than you'd pay for a good motel unit – and you wouldn't face the maintenance worries.

You could make things easier by buying with friends, or renting out the bach for part of the year. You'll normally pay tax on this income but, depending how much use you make of the bach and how long it's rented out, Inland Revenue may regard it has an investment and allow you to claim part of the mortgage interest, maintenance and other bills as tax deductions. (See Chapter nine, "Buying for Investment".)

In a few areas, you'll find developers offering sections for sale, with an attractive financing package that includes interest rates below bank home loan rates.

The real benefit of a holiday home, from a financial point of view, is the potential to make a very handsome tax-free capital gain over the long term. At Pauanui on the Coromandel coast, for example, some property values increased by 40 percent per year through the 1980s.

Location, as ever, is the vital factor. Look at population growth, development planning and proximity to cities. If you resell, a holiday bach within an hour's drive of a growing city will hold more appeal than one which is three hours away. Some holiday homes on larger blocks just outside a built-up area could find that the town comes to meet them; subsequent zoning changes could see property values rise.

Properties directly on a beach or lakefront carry a premium of tens of thousands of dollars above properties that have a road between them and the water.

Freehold title is preferable to leasehold or cross-lease.

In an attempt to maintain and lift property values, some beachside subdivisions put restrictions on what new owners can do. Some, for example, don't permit buildings with fibrous cement walls.

If you buy a bare section, with the intention of spending your summers in a caravan or garage while you save the money to build a house, check out what restrictions the local authority may place on this. Some have specific rules about sanitation if you stay more than just a few days. You may not be able to spend a fortnight in the boatshed after all.

Also bear in mind that buying a block of land doesn't mean you automatically get the right to build on it. Check out your building rights with the local council.

We've seen unserviced blocks of land advertised for as little as $15,000. This may seem incredibly cheap compared with fully serviced sections in a new subdivision. But before you snap up such an apparent bargain, get estimates for having services connected to your section.

If you want a house set back from the road, you could pay $2,000 to $5,000 or more, to have electricity brought to the building. Laying drains to the sewerage system, if there's one there, could cost $1,000 to $1,500. If there isn't one, you'll need a septic tank. Be prepared to pay $3,000 to $5,000 for this. And you'll need water. If you don't have access to a reticulated system, you'll need a tank of around 20,000 litres: allow $2,000. Adding services could cost as much as the land itself.

Even if you like the idea of a classic Kiwi bach, there are options other than buying one. There are baches throughout the country for hire: you can find them in newspaper holiday accommodation columns. There's also been a book published which lists holiday homes available for short-term rental. Some larger unions and other organisations have holiday homes their members can use. Or you could swap homes, privately or through one of the home swap groups which operate in various areas.

At the end of the day, however, the family bach is much more than just a financial decision. It has something to do with the Kiwi ethos and our way of life and love of the outdoors. It's somewhere you can teach the kids fishing and reread the same favourite dog-eared paperbacks. Pick your location and property wisely, and remember that a bach is a spiritual as much as a financial investment.

Holiday home checklist

Once you've decided you'd like to buy and you've chosen the spot, make these checks before you take the plunge:

- [ ] Visit at different times of year, staying for a day or two in a local motel or camping ground. Does the location hold its appeal in different seasons, or is it a desolate, blustery hole for six months of the year?

- [ ] To prevent your holiday arrivals being ruined by discoveries of thefts or vandalism, work out what security you have. Are there permanent residents in the area who keep an eye on holiday properties?

- [ ] If you're buying with an eye to the long term, examine the local rules of development. What could you legally build on the property? If you have visions of pulling down the old bach and building a large retirement home on the property, make sure planning rules will allow this before you buy.

- [ ] Check out what local services are available – dairy, postal services, doctor, telephone, etc. – and prospects for the future growth of these.

- [ ] Consider how long it takes to get there, and whether there's any public transport. You're less likely to make good use of a holiday home if it's too far away for weekend trips.

- [ ] Think about the property's appeal to family members. If children or teenagers would be bored returning to this location for regular holidays, your use of it could be limited.

- [ ] Work out how much maintenance will be needed each year. If the local properties are blasted by sand and salt winds, you could be up for more work than if you bought, say, a lakeside property.

TIMESHARES

When you buy a timeshare, you're buying the rights to spend a week or two each year in a particular accommodation. This may be the same time each year, or it can be floating. If you don't want to use your time, you could rent out the unit to others for that period, or you could swap your time in one resort for time in another, in another part of the country or overseas.

One of the benefits of timeshares is that they're generally built in a prime spot. You get to holiday there each year for a lot less than the cost of a holiday home, you don't have any maintenance to do when you arrive and you often get extra benefits such as the use of small boats.

But don't look at a timeshare as an investment. You're buying a holiday, and you should look at what you're spending – the up-front price and annual charges – as costs rather than an investment which will grow in time.

Let's say you buy two weeks in a unit costing $12,000, with an annual charge of $400 for each week you own. If you didn't buy, assume you could get five percent (after-tax) income on your lump sum. Add that to the $800, and you have $1,400 per year. This, in effect, is what your two weeks are costing you.

But you don't always have to buy new. Timeshare weeks appear for sale in the holiday accommodation columns of larger newspapers. Because you're not paying the promotional costs and developer's margins, you can often expect to pay much less than you would if you were an original purchaser. In August 1996, for example, we saw floating weeks available in Wanaka, Taupo and Mount Maunganui for $3,500 to $5,000.

If a second hand price sounds good, the first things to check are the size of the unit and its precise location. Timeshares can be studio, one bedroom, two bedroom or even three bedroom in size and this is reflected in the price. Generally the smaller units in the less popular resorts are the cheapest.

Marketing scams

Timeshare is a rapidly growing business around the world, but its image is often blighted by marketing scams. Frequently, you're invited to timeshare presentations with promises of a prize for attending. You may not be told it's a timeshare sales pitch. The value of the "prizes" or "gifts" can be highly variable. In the early 1990s, one timeshare promoter was fined $20,000 for offering prizes he had no intention of awarding; another skipped the country before charges could be served. The Consumers' Institute often hears from people who have sat through high-pressure sales pitches, and even signed up, without being told of their rights.

You do, however, have protections under law in the case of primary sales. Developers must either issue a prospectus (under the requirements of the Securities Act), giving financial details about the company, or meet specific terms and conditions designed to safeguard investors' interests. These terms and conditions are given in the Securities Act (Timeshare Schemes) Exemption Notice 1991, together with a schedule of promoters who are exempt.

Among the terms and conditions:

• Units must have been completed and furnished or refurbished.
• A composite certificate of title must be issued to the subscriber.
• There's a five-day cooling-off period after signing the agreement. Within

this period, you can get your deposit back without penalty or deduction.

- Your money must be held in an audited trust account until you're given the specified documents (certificate of title etc.).

- If you want to back out of the deal after the cooling-off period has passed, you can't forfeit more than 10 percent of the full price of the deal.

- Before you enter an agreement, you must be given a written statement signed by the promoters which states, among other things, your rights under the cooling-off period, any exchange rights with other developments, who the promoters are, what the charges and costs are, what the recreational and communal facilities are, and so on.

Copies of the exemption notice are available from Bennett's Government Bookshops for a few dollars.

Secondary sales (resales) by marketing companies are not covered by the prospectus or the Securities Act (Timeshare Schemes) Exemption Notice. Yet the majority of sales in New Zealand at the time of writing are resales. This is an unfortunate loophole in the protection available to consumers.

Private resales are, of course, not subject to these legal requirements.

We recommend you deal with companies which are members of the New Zealand Holiday Ownership Council, a voluntary industry body with its own code of ethics.

Our timeshare checklist:

- Ignore the prizes offered at timeshare promotions. If you genuinely want a timeshare, look at the details of the deal, and not at the extras.

- Don't be rushed. Deal only with companies which let you take away the paperwork and study it for a few days before reaching a decision.

- Think about whether the size of unit being offered suits you, and the type of week: fixed or floating.

- Look hard at the financial details of properties yet to be built. Will your money be held in trust? Who are the trustees?

- Look at the resale potential should you want to leave in a few years. If a nearby resort has been operating for several years, are second-hand timeshares available? What do they sell for?

- Look at maintenance or annual charge costs, ask if these can go up and, if they can, what limits there are on them.

> • Get a lawyer to look over the agreement before you sign. He or she should also tell you about what type of ownership is being offered, such as unit title or lease, and explain the implications of this. For existing properties, ask your lawyer or accountant to look into the financial circumstances of the resort and its management structure.

RETIREMENT VILLAGES

Well-managed and attractive retirement villages can offer friendly and secure living. In larger villages you can get help within minutes if you need it. The units or apartments are often modern and purpose-designed, with no maintenance worries for the residents. But these aren't rest homes: there are often grounds for bowling or croquet, a swimming or spa pool and organised outings. Couples can remain living together longer, even if one person needs greater care.

But you need to buy carefully, and have the paperwork scrutinised by a lawyer with experience in this area. It can be trickier than buying an ordinary house. A village normally offers one of four types of ownership:

• Licence to occupy

This is the most common form of ownership. You don't own any land or buildings and your name doesn't appear on the property title. Instead, you have the right to use the unit for life. Village developers who offer this must have a prospectus. Ask for a copy, and make sure it's available for your lawyer to check out.

• Freehold or unit title

You own your own unit and a share of common area. Promoters don't need to offer a prospectus. Because your name appears on the title deed, you can use the property for security as a loan – and the village operator can't.

• Cross-lease

You own your home and a share of the common property, but no particular part. Cross-lease places some restrictions on what you can do with your property: you must comply with the lease and other leaseholders must consent. Read the lease carefully. They can be restrictive; one, for example, didn't even let a resident keep a cat.

• Registered lifetime lease

Your lease is registered on the title, even though you don't own the freehold.

Money up front, money ongoing

When you move into a retirement village, you pay a lump sum for your apartment, then a regular fee weekly, fortnightly or monthly, to cover services.

The up-front sum is usually made up of two parts. The first covers your apartment. If your unit has freehold or cross-lease title, then this is the sum which buys it. If you're getting a licence to occupy or a registered lifetime lease, then this sum is effectively a no-interest loan to the manager in return for your occupation.

The second part of the lump sum is a facilities contribution or "lifetime rental". This pays for maintenance of shared assets, renovations etc. If you leave the apartment, you may get some of this money back, depending on how long you've been in the village.

An ongoing service fee can run from around $200 to $400 per month for independent units, to cover such expenses as local authority rates, building insurance and staff salaries.

Serviced units provide cleaning, meals and perhaps even things such as bedmaking, but at a much higher cost – sometimes up to $700 per month or more.

This ongoing charge can be increased, or have its scope changed. Some things may no longer be provided, or things which were once provided at no charge may have become available only if you begin to pay. Have a lawyer check the potential for such changes before you sign up.

Our retirement village checklist:

1. Always get a lawyer to check over the paperwork. These can be complex documents – look for a lawyer with some experience in this area. You also need to have an expert – your lawyer or accountant – assess the financial stability of the village.

2. Choose a village where the operator offers a prospectus with full financial details, where a trustee or statutory supervisor is appointed and which is a member of the Retirement Villages Association.

3. Look very hard at your finances to see what you can afford. You need to be able to meet the regular service fee, and cope with increases to it, on top of living expenses.

4. Before you buy, talk to existing residents, and ask to stay in a unit for a night or two before making up your mind. Try out the village facilities.

5. Check out what would happen if you needed temporary help during a short-term illness, or ongoing care, say after a stroke. If the promise of ongoing care is important, make sure you know exactly what's offered. "Proposed" nursing wings may never leave the drawing board; nursing care may be provided at a different location, meaning that you must leave the village and your friends there.

6. If you plan to move to a village, do it while you're still in good health and can enjoy all the facilities. Couples should move in while both partners are in good health.

7. Ask what happens if, after a year or two, you want to move out of the village. What restrictions are there on you selling your unit, or does the manager buy it back? Do you get the capital gain or loss on sale?

SECTION B: *Selling*

11

SETTING AND NEGOTIATING THE PRICE

When you sell your property, you may or may not want to set an asking price. You could simply promote your house hard, and see what prices are offered. Not giving an asking price may put off some inexperienced buyers, but those buyers with a feel for the market can give an indication of a realistic price. You could listen to these opinions and then set a price.

More often, you'll want to name a price where negotiations can begin, or as a guide for tenders.

Whether or not you set an asking price, you'll want to know in your head what price you're willing to settle for. This will depend on your motivation and how urgently a sale is needed.

HOMEWORK

There are lots of different sources of information you can use to help you determine a price:

- Real estate agents are usually very willing to give you an appraisal at no cost. They hope that they'll be selected to sell the property. If you're planning a private sale, let them know this before they do the appraisal – they may still be happy to go ahead, hoping you'll bear them in mind in future. Select an agent who has several years' experience, particularly in your area.

    The agent's estimate of market price may be pitched at exactly the level the agent thinks the market would meet, or it may be pitched slightly higher or lower. Agents may be tempted to pitch high if they think this attractive figure will encourage you to sign up with them. They may pitch low if they think you'll accept that lower figure, and they can get a faster sale.

- Find out what nearby houses have sold for in recent months. You can buy this information from Valuation New Zealand. By itself, this data can help you to estimate your own price, as you make adjustments for the differences in properties.

  ValNet, a telephone service, does something similar. It considers recent sales and other information to give you an estimate of the value of your property.

- If you're willing to spend more, you could get a valuation from a registered valuer.

Before you approach an agent or valuer, you may want to find out what the possibilities are for the redevelopment of your section. For this, you'll need to talk to your local council. But if your property fits the requirements for subdividing or cross-leasing, then this could have a major impact on value. For example, your property may be worth much more to a developer if he or she knows that the little cottage can be removed, and three townhouses built on the site. If this is the case, point it out to the agent or valuer, and ask for estimates of your property as it is, and what its potential is worth.

Before you start working out a price, you'll also need to take a measure of the market. If interest rates are falling, more buyers may be encouraged into the market, for example, and prices may firm. But if a big company decides to close a local factory, your local property market could be hit.

There may also be varying levels of demand in different parts of town. For example, areas close to the city may boom when 20- or 30-year-old suburbs some distance away are out of favour, and vice versa.

And the markets for different types of property may not be the same. You may find more people looking for low-maintenance two-bedroom homes, for example, and a sluggish market for four-bedroom houses on large sections.

STRATEGY

Once you've got this information together, you've an idea of what price the property might fetch. When you're setting the asking price, you also need to take into account:

- How urgently you need to sell. If you're being transferred and you want to settle into your new life quickly, you may be happy to accept the best price immediately available in the market.

- What costs or commissions you're likely to face. If the agent will get $10,000 of your sale price in commission, do you want the price to allow for this? Bear in mind, though, that if buyers think your house is worth $190,000, they're not likely to pay $200,000 just to cover your agent's commission.
- What you're prepared to negotiate in the deal. For example, you may be prepared to accept a lower or higher price for a fast or delayed settlement date.

For most negotiated sales, the seller sets an asking price which allows room for a drop during the sales talks. In this instance, it's important not to set the asking price too low. If you get a strong offer at that price, it's difficult to turn around and ask for another $10,000.

Don't set a figure which is so high that genuine buyers are put off. If you've priced it after carefully considering similar homes on the market, you will not need to negotiate a large amount – $5000 is a realistic margin.

It is less common to set a price as a basis for upward negotiation. To work effectively, this strategy requires good promotion and competition among buyers. It's the basis for tenders, when you ask for offers above a certain figure. It can also apply when you set the reserve price for an auction.

The asking price you set should be approximately what you think is a fair market value. Never deceive buyers by setting a ridiculously low price that you would never accept. If you set the price ridiculously high, you could miss buyers who are looking for a property like yours, but are put off only by an unrealistic asking price.

The condition of your property will also be a consideration when you set the asking price. If your home is in good condition and spotlessly presented, you can obviously ask more than if it needs renovation, or if renovations are only partly completed. If you're in no hurry to sell and you want the top price you can get, consider making small improvements which could help a sale, or consider getting a commercial cleaning firm to work on the outside or inside of your property, and perhaps a professional gardener to bring the garden up to scratch. See Chapter 8, "Home Improvements", for further details.

If you want to sell through an agent, and your agent thinks the price you're asking for is realistic, then you're in business. But what happens if you think your house is worth more than an agent or valuer suggests?

Many people don't have a realistic view of the current market. They assume or hope that their property has increased in value by a larger amount than it actually has. Agents can point to many homes which have been on the market for a long time, because the sellers are unwilling to "meet the market". It's common for people to think their houses are worth more than they really are.

But we're also aware of instances where sellers, unhappy with a valuation or appraisal, have gone ahead with promotion for a private sale, and have sold for a figure above what the professionals told them they could expect. Even if the sale price ends up the same as you would have got through an agent, you're still better off because you don't have the agent's commission coming out of the price.

NEGOTIATING FOR THE PRICE YOU WANT

If you think the written valuation you received is favourable, and you'd be very happy to sell at that price, you could use this as a bargaining tool when negotiating with a buyer. But if you think you can get more than the valuation, then you may wish to keep this to yourself.

Are there any elements of the sale other than price which you're happy to talk about in order to get the price you want? It may be, for instance, that you could leave plumbed-in whiteware in the house. If you haven't yet bought a place to move to, then you may find a financial advantage in getting a delayed settlement date in return for a small concession on the price.

You may be prepared to leave some finance in the property in return for getting the price you want. Discuss this with your lawyer first.

Point out any hidden value in the property. For example, if you know from your enquiries that your section meets the requirements for subdivision or cross-leasing, then this affects its value. Even if the buyer doesn't plan to take advantage of this, you can point out that this will affect resale value for them when they come to move on.

If an agreement is close but that gap of the last few thousand dollars is proving difficult to bridge, ask if the agent would take a reduced commission to clinch the sale sooner. Even though the commission rate has been set in writing in the contract, agents can agree to take a lower amount.

But don't bank on this. If the agent has done a good job, brought you an offer and negotiated the highest amount out of a buyer, the agent may be reluctant to turn around and take a big cut in income.

Our next chapter gives more detail about dealing with real estate agents.

12

USING A REAL ESTATE AGENT

It's common to use a real estate agent when selling a house, but a recent survey of *Consumer* readers showed that only 64 percent of those who had used an agent were happy with the service they received. What's more, only 51 percent of sellers said their agent gave them value for money.

This chapter shows you how to get the best out of your agent. But of course you don't have to use an agent to sell your house (see our chapter on selling your home yourself).

AGENTS AND SALESPEOPLE

By law, all real estate agents must be licensed with the Real Estate Agents Licensing Board and be members of the Real Estate Institute of New Zealand (REINZ). The agent is the person or firm with a licence to run a real estate business. A would-be agent must be appropriately qualified and have three years' practical experience before being eligible for a licence. A real estate salesperson is usually an independent contractor to a particular real estate firm. Most people use the term 'agent' to refer to both the agency and the salesperson. We'll follow that convention here.

You list your property with the agent and sign a listing contract with them. In other words, the contract is between you and the agent, not between you and the individual salesperson.

Good agents can make a decent living from real estate. Some city agents earn annual incomes of $100,000 or more. It's quite easy to become a sales-person, and anyone can decide to give real estate a go. This means you could strike someone very good or someone who's just not cut out for real estate. In fact, 20 to 30 percent of the salespeople who join the industry each year drop out within 12 months.

WHAT A GOOD AGENT DOES

The agent represents you in the selling of your house. Having a thorough knowledge of the local property market, a good agent will appraise your property and discuss with you a realistic asking price. The agent then promotes the house, takes potential buyers through and answers any questions they have.

A good agent is a people person, putting both sellers and buyers at their ease, and screening buyers so that only genuinely interested people visit your house.

Once the offers come in, the agent acts as a sounding board, advising you whether to accept an offer, or prepare a counter-offer. The agent will negotiate with potential buyers until a mutually acceptable agreement is struck. However, because this is an important contract and may contain a number of special conditions inserted by the would-be purchaser, you should also seek legal advice before accepting an offer.

Once the offer is accepted, the agent takes a deposit from the buyer, which goes into the agent's trust account. Once the legal work has been sorted out, the deposit passes to you, less the agent's commission.

THE PROS AND CONS OF USING AN AGENT

There are several advantages of using a real estate agent:

- Go-between. Selling a house is a stressful business, and using an agent means you don't have to deal directly with buyers. Because you're detached from the process, you can consider offers carefully and not be browbeaten by an aggressive would-be buyer.
- Experience. A good agent's experience means he or she can advise you how best to present your house to potential buyers. The agent also knows how to promote properties and how to negotiate a good price for your property.
- Market information. A good agent knows the market, and all agents have access to an up-to-date computer database run by REINZ on house prices and sales. The agent can use this information to help you establish your asking price.
- Many house buyers use agents to find properties. This means that the agent's

office is a focus for buyer enquiries and is the conventional place to sell property.

- With sole agency and general listings, the cost of advertising the property is usually met entirely by the agent. If, however, you want the ads for your property to stand out from the rest, you may be asked to contribute to the cost.

There are disadvantages of using agents:

- The cost. Using an agent costs thousands of dollars, although admittedly you don't pay the commission unless your house is sold.
- Variable quality. Although many agents are very effective and hard-working, there are also those who are incompetent.

DIFFERENT METHODS OF SELLING THROUGH AN AGENT

There are four main ways in which you can sell a property using an agent:

General agency.

You list your property with several agencies but only pay a commission to the agency who sells your property. On the face of it, this sounds ideal, but agents are often reluctant to agree to general agency listings.

To a degree, this attitude arises because the agencies are trying to avoid having to compete with one another. But the agents' reluctance is partly understandable. An agent might not work hard to sell a property if he or she knows that another agent could just come along and sell it from under their nose.

General listing has some disadvantages for the seller too. There may be no concerted attempt to promote the property because no one agency is in charge. Also, you may end up suffering from agent overload: your front lawn can become host to many garish 'For Sale' signs, and your house may feel as though it's constantly full of buyers escorted by agents you don't know and can't keep track of.

Sole (or exclusive) agency.

This is the most common method. You give one agent the sole right to be paid a commission if the house sells. The sole agency period usually lasts from one to three months.

There's something to be said for a sole agency. Everything is focused on one agency to produce the goods and the agency has an incentive to sell your house because it's guaranteed the commission.

One drawback is that a sole agency is a monopoly. If the agent turns out to be unsuitable, you're stuck with them until the sole agency period expires. Another problem is that, if you should sell the house yourself, you may still have to pay the agency commission.

Some sole agency agreements are open-ended: the agreement has an automatic right of renewal or lasts until the house is sold. This means you could be stuck with a useless agent until the house eventually sells or you take it off the market. Don't sign an open-ended sole agency agreement.

Auction.

At an auction, potential buyers bid against each other to buy your property. You place a reserve price on your house. If the bidding doesn't reach the reserve, the house isn't sold.

The property can also be sold before or after the auction under normal sale conditions. This means that, when you sign the auction authority form, you'll also be asked to sign a sole agency agreement.

An advantage of auctions is that the bids are unconditional offers to buy. This means there's no fiddling about with conditional offers, wondering if the buyer will be able to sell their own place and/or arrange finance.

A drawback with auctions is that they must be heavily promoted and the seller usually has to pay for this. The cost varies, but it can be $1,000 or more. In our experience, some of this advertising merely pushes the name of the agency.

As an expert brought to New Zealand by United Realty in 1990 said: "The ultimate aim must be to have sellers pay all costs."

Also, the success rate of auctions is not high. Our research indicates that less than half of auctioned properties sell at auction. We suspect that buyers may not be keen to bid as they know their offers are unconditional.

Tender.

You can organise to sell your house by tender with or without using an agent. You advertise your property and receive written offers, which can be conditional. No potential buyer has an opportunity to see the other tenders. With a closed tender, all tenders must be in by a certain date. Open tenders have no deadline. You don't have to accept any of the tenders submitted.

Once again, you usually must pay for the advertising and the house may revert to a sole agency if no tenders are accepted.

Auctions and tenders are commonly used for houses whose values are difficult to determine, such as unusual properties or those in popular suburbs.

Which is best?

Generally, we believe that you shouldn't put an ordinary house in an ordinary suburb up for auction or tender. It's unlikely to attract much interest and your advertising dollars will have been wasted.

We think sole agencies are the best way to go. The agent has the incentive to sell the place. You should also try to insert a clause in the listing contract allowing you to sell the property yourself without having to pay the agent's commission. Also, negotiate a relatively short period until the sole agency expires: one to two months is best. You can always renew the contract when it expires.

COMMISSIONS

Many people believe that real estate agents' commissions are set by law. This isn't so; commissions vary from agent to agent. When we did a nationwide survey in 1996, we found that the same fees generally apply, irrespective of which method of selling you use.

You usually pay a flat fee plus a percentage of the price for which the house sells (all fees are plus GST):

• The flat fee was usually $300 to $500 (although some agents charge no flat fee at all).

• In some cases, the percentage fee was 3.75 percent to four percent on the entire amount for which the house sells. Often though, a two-tiered system is used. This is usually 3.75 percent to four percent on the first $200,000 to $300,000 of the sale price and two percent on the balance.

So, if your house sells for $180,000, at the top end of the tiered scale, you would be charged $8,662.50. This is calculated as:

$500   +   (.04 x $180,000) = $7700 x 1.125 = $8662.50.

(flat fee)   (percentage fee)   (GST)

It's not hard to see why agents use percentage fees. They're automatically inflation-indexed. As house prices rise, so too do the commissions.

Clearly the commissions are quite hefty, and it pays to shop around. For example, for a $100,000 house in one area of the country the most expensive fee we found was around $2400 higher than the cheapest. But, of course, you shouldn't base your choice of agent solely on price.

The fees quoted are the agents' standard maximums, and there is usually room to negotiate. Our *Consumer* survey found that 39 percent of those who used an agent attempted to negotiate a lower fee. Of these, 38 percent were successful. You can even negotiate after the listing contract has been signed. An agent may come to the party if, for example, a lower fee means that the house will be sold.

Don't forget that if you sell by auction or tender you usually must also pay for advertising.

HOW TO PICK A GOOD AGENT

Shop around. Remember, you're looking for a well-established, hard-working agent with a good knowledge of the local property market and, you hope, a list of potential buyers.

Begin by asking friends and workmates to recommend someone and have a look through the residential property sections of the local papers, as well as handouts such as the Property Press. See which agencies are placing good, eye-catching ads for properties similar to your own.

Ring a few agents and make appointments to go and see them. Mention that you're shopping around. During the interview, check out the office. Is it clean and well presented? Are there good properties similar to yours advertised in the windows? Is the office in an accessible location? Are the staff welcoming and business-like?

Get the agents you meet to sell themselves to you (after all, selling is their job). Ask them how long the office has been in the area, how long they've been in the industry and how many houses they've sold recently. Ask them if they have experience selling residential property. Ask for details of recent local market trends. Are the agents affable, knowledgeable and articulate? Would you be comfortable working with them? If you were a buyer, would you trust them?

Agents should be able to provide references, details of their qualifications, a brief rundown of how they would market your house and examples of the promotional material they would use.

Don't automatically go with an older firm. New firms should be hungry for work, and could very well have, as principals, experienced people who've recently gone out on their own.

Sometimes agents, once you list with them, delegate some of the work to assistants. Ask if this will happen and, if it will, decide whether you're happy with this arrangement.

Appraisals

As part of the shopping around process, you can invite agents to look over your home and give an appraisal of its value.

Compare the values from various agents. If one agent comes in with a value significantly higher than the rest, ask them to justify this. Does their analysis seem reasonable? Don't blindly go with the agent offering the highest value. He or she may simply have overvalued the property. That means it won't sell until you bring the price down. Alternatively, the agent may simply be trying to get you on their books. Once you're signed up and the house hasn't sold, the agent may pressure you to drop your price.

But don't assume the agent's suggested asking price is bang on the nose. In our Consumer survey, 64 percent of people listed for the price suggested by the agent. But twenty percent went for a higher price, and of those, 62 percent got a price higher than that recommended by the agent.

Although you should set a realistic asking price and be fairly confident of getting it, ultimately it's the market that will determine your house's value. If you want a check of the house's value, you can get an independent valuation (see our chapter on valuations).

Listing contract

You should ask the agents you're thinking of using to give you a copy of their listing contract. Different agencies can have different contracts. Read each document carefully, and get the agent to explain anything you don't understand.

Remember that a proposed contract can be altered. Discuss with the agent any clauses you don't like. See if they can be altered or struck out. If the agent won't budge, you might want to go elsewhere.

In one case, where a man was planning to sell a house by auction, he asked to see the contract and was astonished to see that it gave the agent the right to sell the property, at the agent's discretion, before or after the auction. "When I raised my concerns with the agent," the man told us, "he readily agreed to their being struck out." The agency involved has since told us that it's revised its standard contract in light of this episode.

Before you sign a listing contract, make sure that it covers the following issues and that the information is correct:
- The names of the agent and the property owner.
- Details of the property, including its address, legal description, age, dimensions, number of rooms, etc.
- Chattels. Go through this carefully to make sure only the chattels you intend to sell are listed on the contract. Sort out any ambiguities to minimise any chance of misunderstanding between you, the agent and the buyer. For example, you may have a clothes dryer fixed to the wall, which you intend

taking with you. Write on the contract that the dryer is not part of the chattels.

- The method of sale (such as sole agency or auction).
- The agency must produce a written report for you every week detailing how the selling process is going.
- The agent's commission rate. Make sure the commission includes GST.

Don't be rushed into signing. If you're seriously considering an agent, get your lawyer to check the contract out. It won't take long and it's money well spent.

At any stage, before or after having signed the listing contract, you can decide to take the house off the market. The listing contract commits you only to using the agent, not to selling the property. Of course, you can't take the house off the market once you've accepted a buyer's offer.

GETTING THE BEST FROM YOUR AGENT

Never forget that you're the boss. You're paying the agent to work on your behalf. If nothing is happening, demand to know why. Review the agent's regular written reports to you on how the sale process is going.

But you must help the agent as much as possible. Be flexible about letting the agent bring people around. Often buyers will walk into an agent's office wanting to see places right away. Be prepared for lunchtime, after work and weekend visits. Give the agent a key so that potential buyers can be shown through the house when you're not there. Make sure the agent signs for the key and that it's eventually returned.

Lock away or remove any small valuables you have around the house. Some supposed potential buyers may have sticky fingers.

Open homes are a good way of encouraging potential buyers to visit. They don't have to waste time arranging appointments and being ferried around in the agent's car. Open homes are, in some cases, just an invitation for the curious to look around your house without any intention of buying. But, on balance, we think they're worthwhile.

The agent will advertise the open home, which usually run on weekends for two or three hours. It's best if you go out during this time, as your absence makes the environment more relaxing for potential buyers. Tidy up before an open home. Agents have told us how they've arrived to do an open home, only to find they have to wash the dirty dishes first!

Potential buyers are asked to leave their names and addresses. A good agent will use this information to follow up any likely potential buyers.

MISLEADING ADVERTISEMENTS

Every profession has its stereotypical images: with real estate it's the hyped-up advertisement. Everybody knows that the 'handyperson's dream home' is a run-down shack, and a house with 'unique character' is a taste-free zone.

But agents have fallen foul of the law by stretching the truth beyond breaking point. In 1993 the Commerce Commission prosecuted an agency under the Fair Trading Act for an ad which claimed that there was 'not a cent to spend' on the house. The new owners, however, found that many things needed repair. The agent's lawyer argued that the claim was intended as 'merely a puff', but the court begged to differ and imposed fines and costs of $4400.

In a 1996 case, another agency agreed publicly with the Commerce Commission that a newspaper ad it had placed might have been misleading. The ad might have given the impression the property had a beach frontage, when, in fact, there was another block of land between the property and the sea. The agency concerned ensured that all people who contacted it were made aware of the true position of the property and stated that, in future, it would investigate fully claims made about properties.

The Fair Trading Act applies only to those "in trade". So, although an agent can be prosecuted under the act, a private seller (selling their house on a one-off basis) cannot. If, however, the seller gives either the agent or a buyer misleading information about the house, the seller can be liable under common law. You should therefore be scrupulously honest when describing your house to anyone as part of the selling process. If you don't know the answer to a question, say so.

DIRTY TRICKS AND HOW TO COMPLAIN ABOUT THEM

Although most agents are decent people, there are definitely some ratbags out there. Our research has uncovered some of the industry's dirty tricks:

- Encouraging buyers to make low offers. To help prevent this, never tell the agent the lowest price at which you're prepared to sell.
- Turning buyers away. To get a higher commission, an agent may persuade a buyer not to buy your place if the agent thinks that buyer will purchase another higher-priced property.
- Using your place to sell another. The agent may show buyers your house and then take them to a higher-priced, better quality place. The second house looks more desirable after yours.
- Forcing you to sell. Agents may pressure sellers to include fittings they aren't planning to sell (such as expensive light fittings) or to make changes to the

house. In some cases, agents seemed reluctant to argue against buyer's demands in case it jeopardised the sale.

It may be hard for you, the seller, to know if an agent is up to these sorts of tricks. Indeed, we mostly learn about such scams from buyers. To minimise the risk of being conned, try to pick a decent agent in the first place and, if you believe an agent is not acting in your best interests, tackle them about it.

13

SELLING YOUR HOME YOURSELF

Selling your own home without a real estate agent's help is an option which many people find successful and financially lucrative. In a 1996 *Consumer* member survey, out of 1116 people who had bought or sold a house recently, 107 had sold privately and 92 had bought privately. Of the private sellers, 82 percent said they would sell privately again. Almost the same proportion of the buyers would be happy to buy privately again.

Perhaps the biggest bonus is the financial one. With no commission to pay, sellers are left with thousands of dollars – in some cases, over $10,000 – more in their pockets.

And most of the sellers we heard from were happy with the price their homes sold for. The 107 private sellers in the survey received an average 98 percent of their asking price. The 782 who sold through an agent received an average 96 percent of their asking price.

A private sale may be worth considering if:

- You'd like to try to save the agent's commission.
- You haven't had success with an agent.
- You think your house is worth more than the appraisal figure the agents give you. We're aware of cases where people have sold their home for more than the agents said they could expect.
- You haven't owned your home for long, and paying commission would mean taking a loss.
- You like meeting people, you can cope with their reactions to your home,

and you have the skills to judge which aren't serious buyers – not an easy task – and politely rebuff them.

- You like the idea of a challenge and would relish the satisfaction of having done it yourself.
- You're prepared to devote a lot of time to the job, including most weekends.

A private sale isn't for you if you don't want to deal with dozens of strangers coming through your home, you don't want to give up weekends to meet potential buyers, or you just can't be bothered with all the running around and would rather leave it to an agent.

Of course, it doesn't need to be either/or. You could try selling yourself for a month, and if it proves unsuccessful or you realise you're not cut out for it, sign up with an agent. In our survey, almost a quarter of the private sellers had previously tried to sell through an agent, but had no luck there and finally sold the property themselves.

HOW TO DO IT

Practical background work

For a start, make contact with a good lawyer. Your lawyer will have copies of the Agreement for Sale and Purchase of Real Estate form – a standard contract put together by the Law Society and Real Estate Institute. Make sure it's at least the 6th edition, May 1995. The lawyer can fill this out appropriately, or you can do this. Your lawyer can also help you work out the type of sale you would like. With a tender process, the lawyer draws up a tender document, and potential buyers give sealed bids to your lawyer (see page 18 for tender details). There's no negotiating – you simply accept the bid which most suits, or reject all and start again.

But if the idea of haggling over price doesn't unnerve you, you could simply go for the ordinary arrangement of inviting offers, making counter offers, and so on until a final price is agreed on. You could, of course, pay your lawyer to accept the offers and make the counter offers for you.

Whatever the case, your lawyer should only work for you – buyers should use a different lawyer.

You'll need a certificate of title for the property. Your lawyer could get this for you, or you could easily get it yourself for a small charge from the Land Titles Office of Land Information New Zealand (formerly DOSLI, The Department of Survey and Land Information).

You'll also need to work out an asking price, and get a formal valuation done. See Chapter 11 for more details on this process. You'll need to work out what figure you would be prepared to finally settle for. You'll also need to work out what settlement arrangements suit you best. Could you be out in a month, or would you rather have a settlement date beyond then? It's possible for sellers to put conditions in the sale document – eg the new buyers' possession of your home is subject to you buying another house.

Finally, take a close look at your home. Are there any flaws which you could easily rectify? Badly marked lino in the toilet may only cost $100 to replace, but could make $1000 difference to the price. See our chapter on renovations, for tips on jobs you could do which will increase your property's value and buyer appeal. Perhaps you need to hire a small skip and take away all the rubbish off the section and out of the shed and spare room.

Then, look at all your chattels like curtains, dishwasher and the like. Which do you plan to take with you? Which will you definitely leave in the house? And which would you be happy to negotiate over with a potential buyer?

With a lawyer lined up, a certificate of title and valuation at hand, and an asking price and bottom-line price worked out, and the house in top shape, you're ready to start the search for a buyer.

Promotions

You'll need to work out a budget for promotions. You'll want some newspaper advertising; a professional sign for the property; and some A4 sheets giving details, to give out at open homes. We've heard people who've sold after spending just a few hundred dollars on a sign and one or two run-on newspaper advertisements. But even if you need to spend $1,000, before you get a satisfactory offer, if selling privately saves you $10,000 in an agent's fee then you shouldn't begrudge that money.

The best advertising is a sign on your property. Potential buyers often drive around places they'd like to live. Get it professionally made up. A 60cm X 80cm sign with a few words on 3 lines (FOR SALE: Ph Mrs Sutton, ...) will cost around $50 to $80. Most signs of this nature are on corflute, the corrugated plastic board.

Or you could spend around $100 to $140 and get a much bigger sign with more details to whet a buyer's appetite: (FOR SALE: Fully renovated 4brm home, wonderful sun, 788m^2 section. Ph Mrs Sutton . . . . for an appointment to view). Call several signwriters for quotes.

Signs should never say "enquire within". You want to be able to control when people see the property, so they see it at its best. And taking initial enquiries over the phone allows you to give some more details about your home and weed out those callers who aren't serious.

At the same time, it you're planning some open home days, you could get the signwriter to make up some signs saying OPEN HOME with an arrow, which you can put up on main roads near your street.

There are basically two types of newspaper advertising to consider. "Run on" advertisements are those which are word only and appear within the single columns. It's the cheapest type of advertising: in the daily papers, a six line run-on ad will cost from around $12 to $25.

Display advertisements can be over several columns, and may include larger type and even a photograph of the property. A two column, 10cm deep classified with a black and white photo of your house in a Saturday edition of a daily paper will cost from around $100 to over $500 for a single insertion, depending on the newspaper you use.

If you think properties in your area are in hot demand and your place is very tidy with no drawbacks, try placing just a few run-on ads for a start and see what response you get. If that doesn't work – or if you want to reach a lot of people and get the absolute top price you can – go for a display advertisement.

Your advertisement should give the street and suburb, section size and approximate age of the house, special features, number of bedrooms and bathrooms, parking or garaging details, and perhaps a few words about its immediate neighbourhood or location. Keep your descriptions strictly honest.

There is a debate about how much you should stress the fact that it is a private sale. Some people say that knowing this attracts buyers who prefer to deal this way, or are tired of dealing with agents. Others say that it makes some potential buyers nervous. You'll have to make up your own mind.

You'll also need to make up some A4 sheets with information about your home to give to people who look through and to have available on open days. Again, the sheets should be tidy and of a professional standard to give buyers confidence. If you don't have a home computer or a friend who can make them up, go to a secretarial service.

The information sheets should contain all the hard facts a buyer might need to know, with some promotional push of the pluses of the property. You may even include a photograph of the house or view. The sheet should include:

- Section size and house size
- Approximate age of house
- Number of bedrooms/bathrooms
- Other rooms (eg separate dining room, study, second living room)

- Details of recent renovations
- Special features (security system, native timber floors, etc)
- Government valuation
- Brief description of garden
- Parking/garaging arrangements

We reproduce a sample sheet over the page.

As with the sign, all the details here should be strictly accurate. Don't make claims like "subdivision of section possible" unless you've checked that out in advance.

Viewing appointments and open homes

First impressions are crucial. Make sure the lawns are cut, edges clipped, windows and exterior paintwork are clean.

The "feel" of your house will attract or turn off a buyer. Make sure it's clean and tidy. Bathrooms and kitchens in particular should be spotless. If it's impossible to keep it this way all the time, restrict appointments to just to weekends and perhaps one midweek evening. Small children and exuberant dogs could go to grandma's when potential buyers are expected. Putting things away in drawers and wardrobes will make your rooms feel larger.

You may feel it's worth investing in a professional cleaner or gardener to bring your place up to scratch.

Many people recommend having coffee perking in the kitchen, perhaps the smell of baking (which can be faked by warming some vanilla essence in the oven), soft music playing and fresh flowers at several points. Have your best towels out in the bathroom. Make it comfortable and welcoming without being too corny or over the top.

If you'd be delighted to sell for the valuation figure you've received, you may make the valuation available for people to study. If you think you can get more, you may prefer to keep it to yourself.

Whenever someone comes through your house, whether it's a one-off appointment or an open day, ask them to sign a sheet with their name and contact number.

Open homes are well worthwhile. If your place is spotless, consider holding an open home on both Saturday and Sunday. Early afternoon is the best time, and allow at least two hours. Have a good friend in to help keep an eye on people, but allow them freedom to look around in their own time. Easily pocketed valuables should have been put safely away before you open up.

Sample of A4 sheet to give to potential buyers

18 KOWHAI TERRACE, WATERVIEW, WELLINGTON

A superbly renovated four bedroom home on a freehold section with spectacular views

Features:

- 4 bedrooms (master with ensuite)
- 120m² rimu and kauri construction
- Harbour views from sitting room and master bedroom
- Edwardian character intact – high ceilings and tiled fireplaces
- Polished matai floors throughout
- Kitchen renovated with European appliances
- Potential for loft bedroom or hobbyroom
- Professionally installed security system
- Fully fenced, easy care 728m² section
- Off street parking for three cars

Legal Description:

Lot 9 Blk H Deposited Plan 123

Government Valuation and local body rates:

The October 1995 Government Valuation gave a Capital Value of $325,000. However, real estate agents suggest property prices in this suburb have risen approximately ten percent since then. The local body rates for 1996 were $1733.

Location:

Kowhai Terrace is a cul de sac of 18 owner-occupied homes on the western hills overlooking Wellington Harbour. A bus route passes along Tawa Street, two blocks away, and there is also a dairy within two blocks. Two shopping centres are within five minutes drive, and it is approximately 12 minutes drive to the centre of Wellington.

Terms of Sale:

If wishing to make an offer, contact vendor or vendor's solicitor, Mr Tony Gardiner, at Gardiner Windle Harrison, Ph . . . . Deposit of five percent to be paid to vendor's solicitor. Settlement to be negotiated.

Vendors:

Ted and Margaret Corboy, Ph . . . .

You don't have to point out every little flaw. But you should point out things where a buyer could easily be misled. For example, if fencelines are built in the wrong place and your garden is really much smaller than it appears, you are taking a risk if you do not point that out.

The process of selling

You'll need to do one of the more difficult jobs a real estate agent does: check out potential buyers. Who is serious, and who is just sightseeing? Who can genuinely afford your house, and who are wishful thinkers? The answers to these questions will come from talking to the people, asking if they've already sold, if they have finance lined up, what their timeframe for finding a house is, and so on.

If you've chosen to sell by tender, then the key part is promoting your property. You don't have to negotiate over price.

But if you've chosen to consider offers, you have some more work to do. Firstly, you will need to consider if an offer is close enough to what you want to be worth starting negotiations. If so, you accept the offer, but cross out the price, write in a higher price, and initial it. The offer then goes back to the buyer, who may do the same. This process continues until you reach a figure you are both happy with.

The conditions of the sale are also something you need to consider carefully. What date suits you best for settlement? Is it worth accepting an offer conditional on the buyers selling their home, or should you wait for an unconditional offer? You don't have an agent's expertise here, so you'll need to carefully think through the options yourself. Your decision will be based on how quickly you need to sell, whether it is a hot or a cool market, how many people have looked through the house or made offers.

Your lawyer may be able to help with advice. Whatever you do, never ever make a final agreement with a buyer until you've discussed the details with your lawyer.

Using a non-real estate company

If you want some assistance with selling your house, but you don't want to hand over all control to an agent, and pay an agent's commission, there is a compromise. Some companies help you with promotions. They can provide the signs, and perhaps even take the calls.

They can't act as real estate agents – by law, that role is restricted to agents who are licenced with the Real Estate Institute. And the Institute polices its powers vigorously.

The Private Sale Company, set up in March 1994, was taken to court by the Real Estate Institute. The Auckland High Court found in March 1996 that because some of the company's services included the involvement of a success fee, it was therefore acting as a real estate agent, and in breach of the law. However, the judge said if there had not been a success fee, then the company would not have been found to have been acting as an agent.

The Private Sale Company changed its fee structure so that its fee is not a commission on sale, and is still operating – in fact, it is expanding under new owners. The company changed hands in September 1996, and is now trading as Private Sale New Zealand. At the time of writing, its 11 franchisees cover an area of approximately 400,000 homes. The Private Sale New Zealand package includes advertising and handling calls from potential buyers.

The Business and Property Listing Bureau offers a different type of service. It introduces buyers and sellers through an extensive database it holds. Buyers are given phone numbers of sellers, and in many cases buyers allow their phone numbers to be provided to sellers. It produces its own magazine which sellers may choose to advertise in. The Bureau, which has been in business for two and a half years, covers the whole country, with offices from Whangarei to Invercargill.

If you're signing a contract with a company which is poviding assistance with a private sale, make sure the contract specifies in writing exactly what services will be provided. Ask about:

- Signs on the property. Does the company provide them?
- Calls from potential buyers. Does the company screen them? Does it make appointments, or just pass on your telephone number?
- What happens if the house doesn't sell in the contract period?
- The total cost of the service, including GST. This should be clear in the contract.

SECTION C: *After the deal's done*

14

MOVE IT

Finding a new home, and anticipating a change of lifestyle, are the exciting aspects of shifting, but there's little to look forward to in the physical work of the move. Yet sorting out just how you'll shift, which company you'll use and how you'll manage the insurance involved are all crucial to a smooth transition.

QUOTES AND CONTRACTS

What a moving company will charge you depends on how far you're moving, whether the shift includes crossing Cook Strait, whether goods are moved on a weekend or public holiday, the type of access to both properties, the type of goods you're moving and the level of packing required. If your possessions include antique crystal, fine china and large oil paintings, expect a much higher bill.

If you're shifting a very short distance, ask movers for their hourly rate. For jobs going further afield, you can expect a quote based on the cubic metres of goods being moved. As a rough guide, the contents of an average three-bedroom home would fill around 30 cubic metres.

Begin looking for a mover at least two to three weeks before you anticipate making the shift. We recommend you get at least three quotes. It's a competitive industry – furniture removal companies fill 18 pages of the Auckland Yellow Pages.

Give movers a detailed idea of the job required, so that their quotes fairly reflect the work they'll have to do. They will need to visit you and look at your home contents before they provide a quote. You should define the extent of the job you want. For example, do you want the movers to unpack at the other end? Do you want the packaging taken away?

Ask for the quotes to be in writing, with correct and relevant details, and signed. You shouldn't pay more than this agreed amount. Although verbal quotes are also legally binding, it can be much harder to prove what was agreed.

Don't make your final decision on price alone. Find out how experienced the company is, and what it does to protect delicate and valuable items. You should also ask who will do the actual shift, because some companies subcontract work out. If this is the case, make sure you're happy with the subcontractor.

The contract should include:

- The pick-up and delivery dates – there should also be a requirement that you're notified when any delay is likely during the shift itself
- Whether the goods will need to go into storage, and if so, for how long
- Terms of payment
- The insurance arrangements
- Liability for damage or loss, and the period in which claims for damage must be made
- Your responsibilities before removal, such as uncoupling any plumbed-in appliances you wish to take with you and taking down pictures and fixtures such as shelves.
- Mention of any unusually large, heavy or valuable items
- Any special requirement or services: for example, what should be done if access to one of the houses is difficult.
- Whether or not the company will unpack and take away packaging

Finally, make sure that the addresses given in the contract are correct!

You should be there on the day to supervise the packing and loading, but the movers should know their job and be allowed to do it without too much interference. If you have young children or a dog, it may be helpful if they could spend the day with a relative or family friend.

Movers should compile a numbered inventory listing all items being packed and moved. Make sure you get a copy of this so you can check the condition of goods as they're unpacked. You could label the cartons by room, or make a note matching carton numbers to rooms. Don't label cartons by their contents. We know of one case where cartons labelled "Waterford crystal" provided easy pickings for an opportunistic thief at an unknown point during a long move.

If the load is to be split, make sure that essential items go in the first load, and that at least one family member is there to meet it. And work out in advance where you want things to go in the new house. This can save a lot of time and effort in unloading and unpacking.

We've heard of numerous stories where removers have been asked to unload or unpack in the absence of the house owner, and problems have resulted. We recommend always having a family member to supervise. Once the truck has been unpacked, you'll probably be asked to sign a release form. This usually states that you've inspected the goods and that they're undamaged.

Before you do this, make sure that everything has arrived. Have a look at what you can. If any damage is visible, this should be noted on the release form. If you haven't had a chance to unpack some things, note this on the form. You could state: "This release is signed on the understanding that X number of cartons have not been opened and the carrier remains responsible for any damage to or loss of goods contained in them." Never sign a blanket statement that everything is in good order if you haven't had a chance to check.

Payment is usually required in advance. If you pay by cheque, cross it, write "Not transferable" between the crossings, or else get a signed receipt.

Professional moving companies will also be able to arrange pet transportation, house cleaning and transportation of vehicles.

INSURANCE

The Carriage of Goods Act says a carrier must pay up to $1,500 per unit of goods which are lost or damaged while in its care, unless you and the carrier agree to a different arrangement. (It's not crystal clear exactly what a unit is – this hasn't been tested in court often enough to give a single definition a separate item. In some instances, one cubic metre has been considered a unit of goods.)

In practice, you'll find that most carriers use a different contract option other than the Limited Carriers Liability referred to above. Your options are to take all the responsibility for insurance yourself, or to buy insurance which the carrier has arranged with an insurance company.

If you take responsibility for your own insurance, then this means shopping around for extra cover. Standard contents insurance policies cover your goods anywhere in the country, but not during removal by a third party. For moves within New Zealand, expect to pay around 0.5 to two percent of the value of the insured goods. Sort all this out well in advance of the move.

Check whether it makes a difference who packs your goods. In some policies, you have greater protection if your breakables have been professionally packed by the removers. Check also what excess applies – that's the amount of each claim you'll have to pay from your own pocket.

Taking the mover's insurance is a convenient option, if you're happy with the quote, but there are several things to watch for. First, make sure you see the policy in advance, and read the fine print. Second, itemise your goods in advance, with a value for each. What value you use – the "indemnity" value, which is a depreciated value (what it would cost to replace a second-hand fridge, for example), or the replacement value – depends on the cover you're getting. Ask your carrier or its insurance company for details.

Underinsuring could cause problems later. Under an insurance practice called "average", if you write down only half the value of goods (for example, half the indemnity value on an indemnity contract), and pay premiums on that basis, then you may get only half the payment amount.

Make sure you get a copies of all relevant documents.

We've heard from several people who have been given the insurance documents only on the day the packers arrived, and, in these very stressful circumstances, have tried to cope with understanding exactly what protection they've got.

And finally, make sure you know exactly how long you have to lodge a claim after the move. Claims limits of just two weeks are not uncommon. Make sure all your items are unpacked, checked and accounted for before this.

DO IT YOURSELF?

If you're shifting only a short distance and you have the energy, it may be possible to save a considerable amount of money by moving a lot of things yourself, and using one of the companies which can be hired by the hour to move larger items.

You'll have to pack yourself. It could be that one Saturday you could collar some friends or family members, and move a lot of smaller items on several trips using car trailers.

In many parts of the country you can hire a van and two or three people to move things. We've seen advertisements for a truck and two people from as little as $50 per hour.

If you can call on a local sports team, you may not even need the people – just hire a large van or truck. You can drive a truck weighing up to 3.5 tonnes, including load, with an ordinary car licence.

15

HOUSE INSURANCE AND HOME SECURITY

One of the first things you'll want to do when you've bought a house is to protect it. You should arrange house insurance to start from the day of settlement, but home security is also something you can usefully examine during your first days in a new home.

HOUSE INSURANCE

If you're taking out a home loan to buy a house, the lender will usually insist that you have house insurance. Even if you're in the rare and lucky position of being able to pay cash for a property, house insurance is still essential.

There are two types of insurance: accidental damage and defined risk. Most people will opt for the former, which covers you for accidental physical loss or damage apart from certain specific exclusions. Defined risk, by contrast, offers cover just for the disasters listed, typically fire, burglary, storm and flood. Break a window pane, and you're unlikely to be covered.

Defined risk policies are cheaper. They're often the only type of cover available on rented accommodation and holiday homes.

Most policies have traditionally excluded damage caused by gradual deterioration and wear and tear, but a few companies now offer limited cover for this type of damage, for example, for leaks from internal water or waste disposal pipes.

Other things commonly excluded in house insurance policies include theft by a tenant, damage caused by cleaning and settling of the house.

Although an insurance policy protects you from such disasters as fires, floods and storm damage, having house insurance also means that your home is automatically covered by the Earthquake Commission (EQC). This helps you to recover after earthquakes, natural landslips, volcanic eruptions, hydro-thermal activity and tsunami. The EQC covers the replacement cost of your home up to $100,000 plus GST, with an excess of one percent of the claim (minimum $200). Land and retaining walls are covered within 60 metres of the insured building, though not for replacement value. Excess on land and retaining walls is 10%, with a minimum of $500 and a maximum of $5000. Contents (if they are insured) are covered up to $20,000 plus GST, with an excess of $200. Many insurers have top-up cover above these limits, though what is included in this varies, as we explain below.

How to work out what you need

You'll need to collect a few details about your property: the floor area in square metres, including garage, workshop and decks; the construction materials (brick and tile, cedar, weatherboard etc.); the approximate age of the property (pre-war or post-war); and, for a sum-insured policy (see below), the likely rebuilding costs.

All house insurance policies provide the basics. If you live in a modest house on the flat in a small town with a low crime rate, then you'll probably shop on price, assuming that all the policies give you a reasonable standard of cover. But if you want to make sure specific risks relevant to you are covered, ask direct questions, or ask for sample policy documents to be sent out so you can study the fine print. For example:

- If you've invested heavily in garden landscaping, hedges and shrubs, are these covered?
- If your house is below the road, are you covered for the damage which could occur if a stolen or uninsured car leaves the road and comes through your wall?
- If you're planning extensive renovations, make sure you're covered for possible risks. What happens if part of your roof is off, and there's a rain-storm? If you're building a new house, you'll need contract works insurance for this. If you're undertaking renovations, tell your insurance company.
- If you travel frequently, how long can you leave your house vacant before having to tell your insurance company?
- If there are any tenants living in your house, do you have to tell your insurance company?

For people in places at greater risk of earthquake or natural landslip, checking the details of top-up for Earthquake Commission cover is a good idea if your house would cost more than $100,000 plus GST to replace. Many companies offer some top-up cover in their basic policy, but the details can vary. Some, for example, don't cover landslips. Make sure that the top-up cover you buy includes that for the risks relevant to your property.

Value of cover

There are three types of insurance cover by value on the market:
- Open-ended or no-limit replacement cover
- Sum-insured replacement
- Indemnity.

Open-ended replacement policies will rebuild your home to its previous floor area using currently available materials and with no upper limit set on cost. They're usually available only on post-war homes, although some insurers may provide this cover on older properties which have been completely renovated, including new wiring and plumbing.

With a sum-insured replacement, your policy will specify a dollar limit on rebuilding. The company will pay for rebuilding of your home up to this limit. You should check this each year on renewal, although many insurers automatically lift this amount by the rate of inflation.

There's an easy way to work out the likely rebuilding cost of your home. First, find the floor area. Then go to a larger library, and ask to see a recent copy of *New Zealand Building Economist* magazine. This publication carries current costs, per square metre, of building average and above average properties in different parts of the country. Their "standard" house is 94 square metres with weatherboard construction and a corrugated iron roof; their "executive" house is 118 square metres with a 55 square metre basement, a tile roof and better quality construction materials. Costs can vary by over $100 per square metre between regions.

Simply find the figure for the area nearest you, decide whether your house is average or above average in its construction, and multiply the figure by the floor area of your home. Add allowances for the replacement of features such as gates, fences, paths, drives, decks, conservatories, sheds, swimming and spa pools. The figure which appears in your sum-insured replacement policy should be at least this amount.

As an example, let's say you're buying a 115 square metre house in Tauranga. It's better than average, so you opt for the "executive" figure. For the

Bay of Plenty, this is $1,100 per square metre, plus GST (as at August 1996). So the initial figure you may choose to use is $126,500 plus GST, ($142,313), to which you have to add the value of the other features of your property.

Indemnity cover isn't popular and isn't offered by all companies. Sometimes referred to as market value, indemnity is the replacement value minus depreciation for wear and tear. An indemnity policy wouldn't let you rebuild your house. In the event of a total disaster, an indemnity policy payout plus cash from the sale of your section may allow you to buy a similar house elsewhere, but this will depend on your sum insured.

Replacement insurance is clearly the best type of cover to buy. If you can get open-ended replacement on your home, go for that: it isn't likely to cost significantly more.

Some replacement policies will give you indemnity cover only if you rebuild on a different site. This is likely to leave you short of a large part of the rebuilding bill. If you want the choice of rebuilding elsewhere – or if some feature of your site means that, after a storm or landslip, this may be the only option – make sure your replacement policy includes replacement on another site.

Once you've arranged the appropriate cover, make a record of your property. Take photographs of your house inside and out, including special features and especially after renovations. Keep the invoices for new kitchen cabinets or new lighting. These could help if you have to make a claim – they help you prove your loss.

How to shop for a policy

Shop around at least three companies. Since most companies give quotes over the phone, this won't be a hassle if you have at hand all the details you're likely to need, such as the floor area.

You're likely to find some big differences in premium quotes – in *Consumer* surveys, the difference between lowest and highest quotes on the same house is always hundreds of dollars.

It's a good idea to work out at this stage the sort of discounts for which you may be eligible, and ask for quotes based on these. They're not always offered to you automatically. The most common ways of reducing your premiums are:

- Opting for a higher than standard excess. The excess – the amount of each claim you pay yourself – is commonly $100 on house policies.
- Age discounts are available if you're over 50, 55 or 60.
- Package discounts are possible if you bring other insurance – such as

contents, car or boat. (Having both home and contents insured with the same company is a good idea anyway. It saves disputes over which insurer is liable for a particular claim.)

- If you haven't made a claim in recent years, point this out. A few companies offer no claims discounts on house insurance.

- If you have a professionally installed, monitored burglar alarm, some insurers offer a discount.

Ask for the different payment options, and whether any of them have extra costs attached. Some companies allow you to pay the premium monthly or even fortnightly, which helps with your budget – but your total premium may be increased by 10 percent to pay for the privilege.

When providing details for an insurance policy, you'll often be asked if there are any other relevant facts of which the company should be aware. If there's any circumstance which might influence the company in accepting you or declining you as a client, this is the time to let them know. If you make a claim for a house fire, for example, but you didn't tell the company that your teenage son had a conviction for arson, they may decline the claim if they find out.

Reconsider the amount of cover you need, and get new quotes at least every second year – or annually if cost is a factor. It won't take long. What was once cheap may no longer be so.

You should be aware that companies carve the country up in different ways when it comes to calculating premiums. Some may just divide Auckland in two, for example; others divide the city into smaller areas. So if you're buying in Howick and a friend on the North Shore tells you he's found company X is expensive, don't assume the cost will be the same in your area.

Using a broker

You can use a broker to help you find appropriate insurance cover. If you have special needs, a broker could tailor a policy to suit. Brokers are also familiar with such complications as house extensions. They'll handle the administration work of setting up your policy, and most – but not all – may also assist if you need to make a claim.

Often, you won't pay any more to use a broker than you would if you bought insurance cover directly – their income comes chiefly in brokerage from the companies – but some may also charge you a fee.

You could easily check a broker's advice and price by calling a couple of insurers directly yourself, and comparing the cover and premiums they offer with what your broker proposes. Don't always assume that brokers will be cheaper than going direct. The chief advantages of using a broker are getting coverage more tailored to your needs, and getting advice. For example, while some companies have an age limit of five or ten years for replacement cover on furniture and furnishings, a broker will be able to tell you which companies have no age restriction on replacement cover. The difference when and if it comes to making a claim may be many thousands of dollars.

An insurance broker is independent and deals with most insurance companies whereas an insurance agent generally acts for only one or two companies. We recommend you deal only with brokers who belong to one of the professional bodies – the Corporation of Insurance Brokers of New Zealand (CIBNZ) or the Independent Insurance Brokers' Association (IIBA).

Reduce risks

Some people think that, once they've bought insurance, they should make claims constantly to get their money's worth. We think that's the wrong approach – it's likely to lead to higher premiums in the long run. We think you should aim to keep premiums low, through getting the discounts for which you're eligible, and choosing a higher excess, and avoid making claims where the benefit is likely to be very small.

In the next section, on home security, we point out how you can reduce the risks of burglary. But you can also reduce the risk of major fire and other damage.

- Install smoke alarms. These can do more than protect your property – they can save lives. When you're considering security, think about where you should install at least two smoke detectors. They should be mounted on a ceiling or on a wall within 30 centimetres of a ceiling. Put them near bedrooms and living areas, but not in a kitchen where cooking fumes could lead to false alarms. Check at least once a year that they're working.

- Keep a hose with an adjustable nozzle permanently attached to an outside tap in case of fire.

- Inside, a small fire extinguisher containing dry powder can be useful, especially for kitchen fat fires. Buy a one- or two-kilogram extinguisher with ABC multi-purpose dry powder. This will deal with electrical fires, burning liquids such as fat and also solids such as timber, paper or upholstery. Look for a model which meets the New Zealand Standard; this isn't mandatory. The standard requires the extinguishers to discharge for between eight and

12 seconds, and to be able to throw the powder at least two metres. Keep it in the kitchen. If you have a workshop and you use power tools a lot, consider a second extinguisher for this area.

If fire does break out, however, your first priorities should be evacuating the house and alerting the Fire Service.

- On your section, make sure stormwater drains away properly, and make sure you talk to your local council, and get any appropriate consents, before you begin excavating. If part of your land is on a steep slope, consider a planting programme which may help to stabilise the ground.

HOME SECURITY – BEATING THE BURGLARS

In addition to working out your insurance needs, your first few weeks in a new house are the ideal time to think about security. You'll be able to bring a fresh eye to doors and windows, blind spots on your property where a burglar could try to break in without being seen and other security features or gaps. If you've allowed a little extra cash in hand for immediate renovation or redecoration, consider spending part of this on essential security work if it's needed.

These are the basics which are essential to attend to when you first buy a house:

- Fit good quality deadlocks on doors and windows. If you have wooden doors, the best type is a mortice kind, built into the wood rather than screwed on to it. Double cylinder deadlatches or deadbolts are other options. For your own convenience, get all window locks keyed the same, so one key works them all. Louvre window panes should be glued, or a grille fitted over the frame. With aluminium joinery, ask an expert to check that you've got the best possible locks.

- Build friendly co-operation with neighbours. Introduce yourself when you arrive. There may be a formal neighbourhood watch group you could join or start. Your local crime prevention officer or community constable will be able to advise. Or you may just wish to keep in touch with neighbours, telling them when you'll be away and if you'll be having people staying.

- Keep shrubs and hedges close to the house well trimmed, so any attempted break-in would be more visible from the street.

These are useful options to consider:

- Fit outdoor lights with motion sensors. When you're shopping for a security light, consider the area you want the sensor to detect movement; whether you want it to be adjustable to pick up just large objects like cars, or smaller ones like the family dog; whether you want an override so the light can be on continuously; and how long you would like the lights to remain on once they're switched them on. Fit the light where it will get some shelter from extremes of wind and rain, preferably at a height of between 1.8 and 2.5 metres above the ground to get maximum coverage. If there's a risk the light could be tampered with, then you'll have to go higher.

- If you're out much at night, have lamps inside the house on timer switches to keep the house lit.

- Burglar alarms can be bought for a wide range of prices, but the best quality ones cost at least $1,500. We recommend you get some quotes from alarm companies – they won't charge for this – and then have an alarm professionally fitted. Although most have sirens which sound inside and outside the house, you can also have an alarm system connected to a monitoring service through a telephone line. This costs from $1 per day upwards, and means a guard will call at your property when the alarm is triggered. Some house insurance policies allow a small premium discount if you have a monitored alarm fitted.

- If you have an open carport or an open, drive-in space under your house, consider adding walls and a door to close it in. Door openers operated by remote aren't cheap – they start from around $400 to 500, plus installation – but most have a built-in lamp which comes on as you enter, a useful feature for personal security. The openers lock the doors in their closed position.

- Make sure garden buildings such as toolsheds are fitted with locks.

16

IF SOMETHING'S GONE WRONG . . .

What you can do

Your house turns out to be worth far less than the figure your valuer put on it; the bank's charging a fee it didn't mention in its advertising; the timber in your new home is warping, so doors no longer shut properly and windows don't open. What can you do?

If you have a problem, you may be looking for repair work, an apology, for a deal to be reversed, or just some information. Whatever your case, there are a few key approaches which may help:

- Before doing anything, double check that all your facts are correct. Work out what quality of goods or services you could expect, what went wrong, and what your rights are. Decide what you would like to have done about it.
- Keep a written record of your complaint, noting relevant dates and details. Take photographs of poor workmanship and date these.
- Don't wait after you discover a problem: memories can play tricks if you delay.
- Always give someone a chance to put things right before you go elsewhere. They may not be fully aware of your problems.
- Be reasonable. In most cases, just asking someone to correct a mistake is the best approach. If you start holding out for additional compensation, the dispute could escalate. Compensation may be fair, however, if someone else's actions have resulted in a direct dollar cost to you.

- Even if you need to be firm, you should always be polite.
- If you don't get anywhere at a lower level, get in touch with head office.
- Serious complaints are always best put in writing. Keep a copy of your letters. Where you make phone calls, keep a log of the day and time of the call, who you spoke with and what was said.

You almost always have a choice of avenues for following up a dispute – an industry body, or a hearing completely independent of the industry, like a disputes tribunal. There are pluses and minuses with most of these, so you'll want to think about the best option. If money is involved, choose a body which has the power to make binding awards in your favour.

INDUSTRY BODIES

Banks and insurance companies

- Banking Ombudsman: PO Box 10-573, The Terrace, Wellington. Ph 0800 805 950.
- Insurance and Savings Ombudsman: PO Box 10-845, Wellington. Ph 0800 888 202.

Before going to either ombudsman, you must first go through the disputes procedure of the bank or insurance company you are unhappy with. If, after this, you remain dissatisfied, contact the ombudsman.

Both these schemes can hear claims up to $100,000; neither makes a charge on the consumer lodging the claim.

Neither of the ombudsmen can hear claims about general levels of prices, charges or premiums, or commercial decisions. If a bank lifts the interest rates on all its floating-rate loans, for example, you can't go to the ombudsmen.

The ombudsmen can make binding awards, but they first try to resolve a problem informally. They can award compensation except for indirect losses.

All the major banks are part of the banking ombudsman scheme; at the time of writing (September 1996), the only major insurer to remain outside the Insurance and Savings Ombudsman scheme is NZI Insurance, which has its own independent arbitrator.

Building professions and trades

Building professionals like architects and engineers often have professional associations which offer complaints procedures. Usually, they cannot award compensation, however. You may be better off dealing directly with the professional involved, or taking legal action against him or her, particularly if they have indemnity insurance which covers the problem.

A number of building trade associations, such as the Master Builders' Federation, Master Painters' Association and Master Plumbers' Association, provide an inspection and complaints procedure for disputes involving members' work.

If you've received sub-standard work from a member of the NZ Master Builders' Federation (PO Box 1796 Wellington), that contractor will be required to remedy the work, or the federation will get another member to fix the problem.

If a building problem arises within ten years of a Code Compliance Certificate (CCC) being issued, and you can prove that the problem was a result of the building officer's negligence, you can claim compensation.

Lawyers

• In the first instance, contact your District Law Society.

There are 14 District Law Societies around the country: you can find details in your phone book, or from any law firm. The Society will ask for a response to your written complaint from the lawyer concerned. The complaint may subsequently be referred to a district disciplinary tribunal.

Cases of serious misconduct go to the New Zealand Law Practitioners' Disciplinary Tribunal.

Complaints about fees should be made within six months of receiving the bill. You can only complain to the Law Society if the bill is unpaid or has been paid by deduction from money the lawyer has held for you in a trust account.

If you're dissatisfied with a decision about a fees complaint you can appeal to the Registrar of the High Court within 14 days.

The Law Society has a fidelity fund for compensation for theft by lawyers.

Real estate agents

• Real Estate Institute of New Zealand, PO Box 5663, Auckland.
  Ph 09 356 1755.
• Real Estate Agents Licensing Board, PO Box 5570, Auckland.
  Ph 09 520 6949.

If you have a problem with a real estate salesperson, begin by speaking to the salesperson concerned. If that doesn't resolve your problem, talk to the manager of the agency.

If you're still dissatisfied, you can complain to the Real Estate Institute. The Institute has legal powers to discipline its members for breaches of its code of ethics or rules of practice. REINZ also has a fidelity fund which is used to protect buyers' deposits placed in agents' trust accounts, but for nothing else.

In certain circumstances, complaints can also be heard by the Real Estate Agents Licensing Board. The Board can suspend members and refuse to renew their licences.

Neither body can award compensation to consumers.

Retirement Villages

- Retirement Villages Association, PO Box 345, Manurewa, Auckland.

Each village which belongs to the Retirement Villages Association has a disputes resolution procedure. Try that first. The Association also has a review authority for disputes which cannot be resolved within a village.

Valuers

- NZ Institute of Valuers, PO Box 27-146, Wellington.
- Valuers Registration Board, PO Box 5098, Wellington.

All registered valuers must belong to the Institute. It has a code of ethics and will investigate written complaints about a valuer's conduct.

If you remain dissatisfied, write to the Registration Board. This body can fine valuers. A valuer who is found to be negligent can even be deregistered.

Neither of these bodies can award compensation.

LEGAL ACTION

If you're seeking compensation, costs or damages, many of the bodies mentioned above will not be able to help. You'll need to look at action in a court or disputes tribunal.

If the amount involved is just a few thousand dollars, you don't need a lawyer – you can contact a disputes tribunal and present your own case.

At the time of writing this, disputes tribunals can hear claims for up to $3000, or $5000 if the other party agrees. (These figures are expected to rise to $5,000 and $10,000 in 1997). Their findings are binding and enforceable. It costs $10 to lodge a claim for up to $1000, and $20 for claims above that.

Tribunals try to settle disputes on the principles of natural justice. They are not obliged to stick to the letter of the law. The tribunal hearing are held by referees, who are chosen for their common sense rather than any legal background.

Tribunal hearings are private. You should bring all the documentation you may need with you, and you can also bring witnesses to support your claim if relevant. You may need expert testimony to support your claim, for example a letter from a building consultant stating that they have inspected the site and the work is not up to standard.

Tribunals can hear disputes on most topics, but not in the areas of tenancy or land ownership. There are some other restrictions: for example, they cannot be used as a debt collection agency.

To contact a disputes tribunal call the number in your phone book for your district court.

If larger sums are involved, your first step will be to make an appointment with a lawyer. Ask for a quote (including GST) for just half an hour of his or her time to give you an initial opinion. This could give you some basic information about your options, and the likely costs involved of taking things further.

Another option, if the party you have the dispute with agrees, is to go to arbitration. The Arbitrators and Mediators Institute of New Zealand (PO Box 1477 Wellington) can give you the names of local arbitrators or mediators with relevant experience, and details about what arbitration or mediation involves.

GLOSSARY

Bridging finance
A short term loan, frequently used to provide money to buy one house when a longer term loan is still to be arranged or the proceeds of another house are not yet available.

Certificate of title
The document which sets out the legal description and ownership of a property, and details other property rights concerning that land, eg easements.

Chattels
Drapes, light fittings, carpets and other moveable items in a house. Chattels are not normally included in a mortgage valuation.

Code Compliance Certificate (CCC)
A certificate issued by a local authority building officer or other certifier which states that building work meets the requirements of the Building Act.

Company title
The flat or office owning company issues a Licence to Occupy to a holder of shares in the company.

Conveyancing
This used to mean just the transfer of land ownership, but is now used in a wider context which includes other dealings with land rights such as leasing and mortgaging of land.

Covenant
A legally binding agreement. For example, ownership of a block of land may come with a covenant which prohibits the owner from felling native trees on the property, or from erecting a particular type of building.

Cross lease
You own a share of the land and lease the buildings.

Depreciation
The reduction in value of a property due to wear and tear etc.

Easement
A right for someone who is not the owner of a property to have a certain use of all or part of it. Easements may allow one person access to their property through another property, or may allow for pipes or cables to be laid across your property.

Equity
That part of a property's value which an owner holds after debts are accounted for. For example, if your property is worth $200,000 and the mortgage balance is $125,000, your equity is $75,000.

Freehold
Outright ownership of property, but subject to rates and taxes. Government also holds

the right of compulsory acquisition. Freehold is also referred to as "fee simple". Despite common usage, freehold does not mean mortgage-free.

Gearing
Using borrowed funds to buy an asset. If you borrow a large proportion of the cost of an investment property, for example, you are "highly geared".

Indemnity insurance
Insurance cover which reinstates you to the position you were in before the loss. "Indemnity" is sometimes referred to as market value, and is the replacement value minus depreciation for wear and tear. If a second hand fridge is destroyed in a fire, an indemnity policy will replace it with another second hand fridge.

Joint tenancy
Two or more people own land in a way where the share of one person, on their death, automatically passes to the surviving owner(s). Compare with "tenants in common" below.

Land Information Memorandum (LIM)
A report produced by a city or district council which details what the council knows about the property. This may include consents, rates owing, drainage systems, flooding problems, instability of the land, etc.

Leasehold
Property held for a certain period under a lease document. At the end of the period, the lease may be renewed or the property may pass back to its owner.

Licence to occupy
You have the right to use a property, although you do not own it and your name does not appear on the title.

Mortgage
A charge over a property to secure payment of a loan.

Mortgagee
The organisation or individual who lends you the money to buy the house - usually a bank, life insurance company or the like.

Mortgagor
The person who has borrowed money secured against a property.

Negative equity
The value of a property is lower than the amount of debt owed on it.

Negative gearing
Where borrowed money is used to buy a property, and the annual outgoings including interest are more than the rent earned from it.

Principal
The amount of money you've borrowed to buy a property.

Project Information Memorandum (PIM)
A report produced by a city or district council which details features of the land known

to the council, such as flooding or subsidence problems, stormwater systems, and any statutory authorisations which need to be obtained before building work commences.

Reducing mortgage
You pay back an equal amount of principal each time, with the balance of your payment going towards interest. As the principal you own is reduced, so the interest you pay reduces. Instalment amounts therefore decline with time.

Sole or exclusive agency
A contract with a real estate agent which allows only that company to sell your house. Some sole agency contracts still allow you to sell privately, some stipulate that the agent gets commission even if you make the sale yourself.

Table mortgage
You repay the same regular amount over the life of the mortgage. At first, most repayments cover interest, but over time more and more of each instalment goes to paying off principal.

Tender
Intending buyers make sealed written bids. The seller can accept the best bid or reject them all. "Open" tenders have no deadlines; "closed" tenders ask for bids to be in by a certain date.

Tenants in common
Where two or more people own property in distinct shares and, on the death of one owner, ownership of that person's share goes to their heirs, and not automatically the surviving owners. Compare with "joint tenancy" above.

Timeshare
A property is divided into units which allow occupation rights for typically a week or more each year. It may be the same period each year, or a "floating" period.

Torrens System
The system of registration of land title adopted in New Zealand, sometimes referred to as the Land Transfer system. Boundaries are carefully recorded, and ownership is recorded in a title held at the Land Titles Office. Laws relating to land in New Zealand are not the same as, for example, those in England.

Unit title
Flats or apartments are individually owned but common property (usually stairs and driveways) is owned and administered by all the flat owners together through the body corporate.

Vacant possession
There are no tenants in the property and it is not leased out.

Vendor
The seller of a property.

INDEX

Money saved

or your money back.

It's a fact — just one piece of advice from CONSUMER magazine can save you the cost of a subscription! We test everything from dishwashers to dryers. We alert you to shoddy products and the traps that cost you money. Then we help you hang on to the money you've saved with no-nonsense, independent advice on savings, insurance and investment. Subscribe today and have CONSUMER delivered eleven months of the year. And if you don't agree that you've saved money, time and frustration we'll refund your money in full. What could be fairer?

CALL OUR 24-HOUR TOLL-FREE SUBSCRIPTION HOTLINE:

0800 CONSUMER
2 6 6 7 8 6

The best tool

for your home and garden.

With *CONSUMER HOME & GARDEN* you'll get a lot more than expert gardening guidance and practical advice on a wide range of home improvement topics. You'll also have the "inside knowledge" you need to make informed choices and avoid expensive mistakes. That's because our regular test reports give you brand-name ratings and help you buy the best product for the job - whether it's power tools or potting mix, house paint or fertiliser. Subscribe now, and have *CONSUMER HOME & GARDEN* delivered every second month.